FOSSICKING AFAR

Joseph A C Mazzucchelli

17.1.1842 – 16.5.1909

by

Richard Mazzucchelli

COPYRIGHT NOTICE

© Richard Mazzucchelli, 2022

All rights reserved by the author. This book is copyright. Apart from any fair dealing for the purpose of private study, research, criticism or review, as permitted under the Copyright Act, no part may be reproduced by any process without written permission from the publisher.

No part of this book may be used or reproduced by any means, graphic, electronic, or mechanical, including photocopying, recording, taping or by any information storage retrieval system without the written permission of the copyright owner except in the case of brief quotations embodied in critical articles and reviews.

The views expressed in this work are solely those of the author and do not necessarily reflect the views of the publisher and the publisher hereby disclaims any responsibility for them.

A catalogue record for this work is available from the National Library of Australia

ISBN (sc): 978-0-6451627-7-6

Published by Footprints Publishing Pty Ltd

Printed by: iPrintPlus

Cover photo supplied courtesy of the Shire of Coolgardie

Dedicated to the Memory of

Mr A C (Corry) Marshall,

who always thought I had a book in me

TABLE OF CONTENTS

1. Switzerland - 1859	1
2. Ballarat - Victoria, 1860	22
3. Stawell - Victoria, 1860 to 1863	36
4. New Zealand - 1863 to 1865	66
5. Stawell - 1865 to 1871	84
6. The Hanoverian Reef - 1871 to 1872	97
7. The Miners Rest Hotel - 1873 to 1878	102
8. Swiss Farm - 1878 to 1887	112
9. Stawell - 1887 to 1898	118
10. Coolgardie - 1899 to 1901	132
11. The Last Foray - 1901	163
12. Redemption - 1901 to 1909	179
Epilogue	197
Acknowledgements	202
Bibliography	203

1

Switzerland - 1859

It is only mid-afternoon; the westering sun is already casting deep shadows throughout the Val de Poschiavo and the air is chill. From his vantage point high on the Bernina Pass, Giuseppe can see the coils of smoke rising from the chimneys of Poschiavo far below and, a mile further to the south, the village of Prada, where his family lives. He gazes intently, seeking to imprint on his mind the scene before him, knowing he may never see it again. The steeples of the Catholic and Evangelical churches of Poschiavo stand out clearly above the grey stone houses huddled within the narrow confines of the valley, split by the fast-running river which waters the puny strip of arable land between the town and the emerald waters of Lake Poschiavo. Beyond the gap, on the far side of the lake, lies the southern border of Switzerland with what is yet, but soon, to become the unified country of Italy. Dark green pine forests clothe the steep flanks of the mountains on either side of the valley, but here and there, cleared patches of yellowish, lettuce-green mark alpine meadows wherever gentler slopes allow. To any objective observer, the scene before him is one of great beauty but Giuseppe has a restless spirit. He yearns to explore, not just different parts of the world but different ways in which he might live his life. Much as he loves the mountains of his birthplace in south-eastern Switzerland, he knows his destiny lies elsewhere.

Summer is over and tomorrow he will return to Prada with the cattle he has been minding in the high country for old Vanzetti. And in another month, he will leave for his new life in Australia, in the British colony of Victoria. He knows there will be arguments and entreaties before he can leave. Although his father will be indifferent, his mother dearly wants him to stay and he will have to brace himself against her tears and those of his sisters. Throughout the summer he has pondered and weighed the pros and cons of his decision and there can be no turning back now.

He can hear the dissonant bells of the herd behind him as they seek what is left of the grass on the alpine meadow around Lago Bianco. But it is late in the season and what remains from the summer grazing is becoming ever more shrivelled by the nightly frosts. He turns away from his reverie and busies himself with the task at hand, herding the cattle into the stone enclosure where they will huddle together for warmth during the cold night ahead. Then he will prepare his evening meal and settle down to sleep in the slab herdsman's hut for the last time. Vanzetti will only pay a pittance for his summer's work, but it is critical he completes his task and top up his savings to pay for his passage to Victoria.

It is more than a year since his older brother, Matteo, left for Victoria, sailing from Liverpool in England on the *Scottish Chief*. The family has received only one brief letter from him since his departure and that had provided little information. It seems the long sea voyage had been 'difficult.' There had been conflict between the passengers and crew. After arrival in Melbourne, he moved to a place called Pleasant Creek, where people were reportedly finding gold but he hadn't found any himself. He had sent his love and that was it.

Matteo was never one for writing letters or reading, for that matter. Born five years before Giuseppe, Matteo is as gregarious as Giuseppe is reserved and shy. Matteo is quick to make friends and enjoys the company of others.

Giuseppe, like everyone else, loves Matteo but can't help feelings of envy. After all, it was he, Giuseppe, who had provided Matteo with the idea of far-away Victoria as the place to go when he had to leave. At this time, the late 1850s, many young men are emigrating from Poschiavo, mainly because of lack of work and opportunity. Political turmoil in the area just a few miles to the south, soon to become part of Italy, has added fear of conscription for the young men of Poschiavo. Matteo had an additional reason to leave. He was apprenticed to his father, a stonemason, but the relationship was fraught and culminated in a furious argument, with both parties vowing to never work together again. Giuseppe had wanted to leave with Matteo but had only been 15 at the time and was persuaded by his mother to wait another year. He is no longer prepared to wait. If he is going to succeed in prospecting for gold, he has to leave soon or forget it forever.

The seed for the idea to migrate to Victoria had taken root in Giuseppe's mind in the summer of 1857, which he had spent minding Vanzetti's herd in the alpine meadows. Giuseppe started minding cattle in the alpine pastures over the summer, at the age of thirteen. Nervous of the responsibility at first and uncomfortable in the rough company of the older herdsmen, many of whom were disreputable types from the valley, once he observed how others went about the task, he started to enjoy the solitude and freedom of his time in the mountains. The majestic alpine scenery of the Bernina Pass lifted his spirits, not just the snowy mountain peaks, d'Arlas, Cambrena and Lagalb, but the wildlife and the delicate plants growing in the more sheltered areas fascinated him. Giuseppe was even fascinated by the variety of the rocks he observed.

In successive years, he explored more of the crags surrounding the alpine meadows while the herd grazed, becoming familiar with areas where unusual rocks, fossils or plants could be found. With little understanding of the features he was seeing, Giuseppe wished he could meet someone who could explain the significance of his observations. Pondering the processes that shaped the topographic features, he kept an inventory in his head of unusual rocks and places and appreciated the time to reflect on his home-life. Giuseppe loved his mother but loathed her efforts to direct him into a career as a priest. It was only her desire for this prospect that allowed him to remain at school and continue learning. When he was fifteen he told her he had no intention of joining the church but she persisted, no doubt hoping he would change his mind. For Giuseppe, this meant he could continue learning at school. Hating confrontation, he studiously kept out of the frequent arguments between his mother and father, brother and father and amongst his sisters. He analysed the issues which prompted family conflict but preferred to keep his thoughts to himself.

That summer he met an English naturalist in a party of hikers travelling southwards up to the Bernina Pass from St Moritz. The Reverend Ernest Brenton was one of four sons born to a titled, well-endowed English family. As was the custom at the time, his oldest brother would inherit the family estates and title, so the younger sons needed to find a career. Only a few callings were open to a gentleman. Most chose a military career, particularly those from families with sufficient wealth to purchase a commission. The brighter minds gravitated towards a profession; the law for those with a theatrical bent, medicine for those with humanitarian leanings. Ernest Brenton found neither of these callings appealing, being more interested in the big questions: the origins and meaning of life itself, so he took the logical steps towards a career in the Church of England.

Once established in a parish, which supplied a living and a lot of time and freedom to pursue other interests, Ernest, like many other clergymen, such as John Stevens Henslow, mentor to Charles Darwin, developed an active interest in natural science. This took him on ever more far-ranging expeditions, observing all aspects of the natural world. One of the many clergymen who were pioneers of the sciences of geology, botany and zoology, Ernest was interested in exploring and documenting all aspects of God's creation.

That same summer, Reverend Brenton travelled to St Moritz and spent his days hiking in the mountains, making notes and sketches of rock formations and flora and collecting specimens. Each day he engaged one or more local guides to accompany him, carry equipment, food and samples and assist with translation. Although competent with the German and French spoken in the northern parts of Switzerland, he was less familiar with Italian spoken in the valleys to the south of St Moritz.

One day, Brenton's party travelled by horse-drawn coach as far as Lago Bianco, atop the Bernina Pass. From there, they headed south-west, on foot, to inspect the glacier descending from Mt Cambrena. Working their way over the saddle below Mt d'Arlas to see the eastern tongue of the snowfield, they came across Giuseppe, tending his herd in the upper reaches of the Val d'Arlas. The boy observed their slow approach, stopping from time to time to examine rock exposures and alpine plants. When Brenton's party was within 600 feet of where Giuseppe sat eating his lunch of bread and sausage, they stopped, clearly excited, to examine scree below a low crag, where Giuseppe had earlier seen fossil fragments.

In appearance, Ernest Brenton stood out in stark contrast to the stocky mountain men who accompanied him, a tall, gangly figure dressed in a long tweed coat and deer-stalker cap. Giuseppe sensed these men might be interested in the things that intrigued him during his long stints in the mountains. He hesitantly approached the group, some of whom were sifting through the scree for fragments of ammonites, the spiral shells of the ancestor to the pearly nautilus, which roamed the seas some 150 million years ago. Brenton, meanwhile, was combing the low crag of grey siltstone, looking for the rock layer from which the fossils were shedding. He used a hammer to split several rocks, apparently without success. Giuseppe realised what had attracted their attention and volunteered to one of the Swiss guides that he knew a better location, where complete fossils could be found. This information was translated for the benefit of Brenton, who turned to meet the Italian-speaking youth. Brenton could see that here was a youth with keen powers of observation and a lively curiosity. Giuseppe was short in stature but not stocky like many men from this area. He had inherited the lean physique and fine facial features of his father. His eyes were grey, intelligent and although his clothing was basic, it was clean. The Englishman, Giuseppe saw, was anything but ordinary, pale pinkish skin, wispy blond hair, protruding eyes, small thin-lipped mouth and a quizzical expression. When Brenton spoke, his voice was deep and sonorous, ideal for projecting sermons in a cavernous church. Through his translator, he requested that Giuseppe guide him to the spot where these fossils were to be found.

Giuseppe mounted the small bluff behind them and led the party upwards along the ridge towards Mt d'Arlas. Brenton observed they were following the same stratigraphic horizon that contained the fragments first located. At one point, the ridge narrowed to a rocky path perched between two steep scree slopes. Giuseppe turned to warn the party to watch their step just in time to see Brenton step off the path and start sliding down the scree slope. Brenton had the presence of mind to outstretch his arms and legs and came to rest only a few metres below the path but then his attempts to climb back up the slope only resulted in him sliding further down. One of the guides took a rope from his haversack and hurled one end down to Brenton. With one end anchored, he was soon able to regain the path. Brenton appeared to regard the incident as comical and laughed at his own clumsiness. Giuseppe thought *he's human after all*. Some 300 yards on from Brenton's fall, Giuseppe stopped and indicated a low mound of shaly rubble at the base of a steep cliff. He stooped to pick up a rock he had seen and discarded on a previous visit and proffered it to Brenton. It contained a good ammonite specimen. Impressed, Brenton cast around for similar pieces. Looking up at the cliff, he observed a dipping line of muddy nodules in the bedding of the black shale exposed in the cliff. Brenton worked his way along the base of the cliff to where the inclined bed was within reach and began to crack nodules open with his hammer. At the fourth attempt, he gave out an exclamation of delight. Neatly encased within the nodule was a perfect ammonite, its ribbed whorls a metallic grey sheen contrasting with the earthy texture enclosing it. After an hour's fossicking, the guides' sacks were weighed down with a variety of fossils and Brenton set about sketching the cliff face, indicating where the different specimens had come from. By then it was late in the day and the party decided it was time to head back to Pontresina for the night. Before leaving, Brenton enquired, through the interpreter, whether Giuseppe could guide them to other similar locations where fossils could be found.

Over the next week Brenton returned daily, with just the one local guide who could translate Giuseppe's Italian, to spend time looking at all the places where Giuseppe had observed fossils.

Brenton explained to Giuseppe the latest theories concerning fossils; that they were the skeletal remnants of ancient marine animals which were deposited within sediments on the ocean floor. How they became exposed in mountains, nearly 10,000 feet above sea level and over 100 miles from the coast, was testament to the huge upheavals undergone by the earth's crust.

Naturalists all over Europe, many clergymen like himself, were documenting the different types of fossils and finding the same combinations of fossils could be found at different places hundreds of miles apart. Brenton had observed the same fossils they had found here, far away in Dorset, on the south coast of England. It seemed the different combinations of fossils could provide a means of cataloguing and even determining the ages of the rock strata in which they occurred. Some bold investigators even suggested the rocks themselves may prove to be many millions of years old. This was a problem for a clergyman like himself. He was beginning to doubt the biblical creation story according to Genesis.

Giuseppe showed a lively appreciation of these ideas and became an active participant in Brenton's documentation of the geology of the Bernina Pass area. While Giuseppe's herd grazed in the Val Minor at lower altitude, where the grass was still green, the party explored the lower slopes of Mt Minor and Mt Lagalb. At one point, Giuseppe drew Brenton's attention to an outcrop of rusty rocks bordering a narrow vein of white quartz, which had made him very curious. Brenton picked a particularly heavy brown rock from the margin of the quartz vein and cracked it open with his hammer. Encased within the rusty iron oxides were specks and seams of a yellow metallic mineral. He showed Giuseppe, who exclaimed, 'Oro (Gold)!'

'No,' said Brenton, 'This is just pyrite, iron sulphide or fool's gold but if there *was* any gold in these mountains, it would probably occur in rocks like these. One way to check if there is any gold around here is to pan the sediments in the nearest stream.'

He went downslope with Giuseppe and reaching the stream, placed a handful of the sandy sediments in a shallow metal dish. Adding stream water, he slurried, stirring the mixture with his fingers, then swirled the water with a rotating motion, so the water became murky with the clay dislodged from the sediment. He tipped out the murky water and replaced it with clear stream water, repeating the swirling and shaking of the dish. Every now and then he would scrape off some of the coarse sand at the top of the dish. This procedure continued for several minutes, until the water was clear and very little sediment, mostly dark in colour, remained in the dish. Brenton angled the dish so the remaining sediment formed a band along the join between the base and sidewall of the dish. He rolled this back and forth and Giuseppe observed that it separated into grains of different colours. Brenton took a magnifying glass from his pack and examined the grains intently, focusing on the trailing edge of the band of mineral grains. After a while he handed the dish and glass to Giuseppe.

'What is left in the dish is the heavy minerals. Most grains are black; they are iron oxides, magnetite and ilmenite. You can see the grains of pyrite shed from that vein up the hill. They are the brassy yellow ones. If there was any gold, it would be right at the back, behind the pyrite. You would know if you saw it by the difference in colour and shape.

Gold grains are usually rounded, compared to the pyrite, which has flat crystal faces.'

Giuseppe was engrossed. He could see Brenton had concentrated the heaviest of the minerals in the stream sediment, which would include any gold, the densest of all minerals. He also became aware that with careful observation, it was possible to distinguish between the multitude of different minerals which make up the rocks of the earth.

'I doubt if there would be enough gold in this area to be payable but I would like to check out any other locations where you have seen the same kind of rusty rocks.'

Over the course of the next few days, Giuseppe and Brenton visited several locations where quartz veins and rusty rocks were in evidence. Together they panned many dishes full of stream sediment, but although they saw a few tiny grains they suspected might be gold, they were so fine and sparse they couldn't be sure. All the time, Giuseppe plied Brenton with questions about gold and how to recognise the different minerals they found in the outcrops and panned concentrates.

'You should go to Victoria,' Brenton said at one stage. He went on to describe the recent history of gold discoveries in Australia, transforming the former convict colonies into bustling, wealthy places.

'Apparently, men are finding enough gold to make their fortunes. If we did the same work we did here but in Victoria, I imagine you would have a bag full of gold to take home to your family.'

Giuseppe was intrigued. 'What is this Victoria?' he asked. 'Where is it and what can you tell me about it?'

'Well, it's part of Australia, far away on the other side of the world. It is a very big continent, bigger than all of Europe. Most of it is still unexplored.'

'Do they have farms there?' asked Giuseppe.

'Of course. Some of them are very big, far bigger than in Switzerland, with more than 5,000 sheep.'

Giuseppe was astounded. Such a flock of sheep was unheard of in Poschiavo. What was the term for 5,000 sheep? Surely not a flock! He could never hope to own a farm in the Poschiavo valley but if he could find enough gold, he might be able to buy a farm in Victoria, a bigger farm than old Vanzetti's, even bigger than the biggest farm in the valley.

From that day, Giuseppe decided, even became obsessed, with the idea he would emigrate to Victoria. Brenton's story of the wealth to be made from gold prospecting in Victoria was soon confirmed by news emanating from the neighbouring canton of Ticino. Two adventurers, Giovanni Palla and Tommaso Pozzi, had left the Valle Maggia as penniless migrants and returned two years later as rich men. It was learned they had made their fortunes by digging gold in Victoria, where gold nuggets could supposedly be picked up like pebbles. Giuseppe shared his enthusiasm with his older brother Matteo, who shared it with *his* friends. After two years spent finding out as much as he could about Victoria, Giuseppe was frustrated that Matteo had preceded him and emigrated to Victoria the previous year. But now Giuseppe's plans were set and he was about to put them into action.

At the time of Giuseppe's departure in 1859, the Italian-speaking residents of the alpine valleys of Switzerland were experiencing great hardships, especially the Val Poschiavo. There wasn't enough arable land in the valley to support the rapidly growing population. Crop failures year after year had led to food shortages. Most of the farming land was owned by absentee landlords from the Germanic northern cantons and as a result of the successive poor seasons, the owners were reluctant to spend more money on their farms. The tenant farmers still had to pay rent to the owners, often leaving them with barely enough to live on. The short growing season in the alpine valleys meant the menfolk were used to spending up to six months each winter, away from home, working as labourers or mercenary soldiers in Venice and Lombardy.

The 1850s brought two additional factors to the fore. The political environment throughout the whole region was one of extreme turbulence. The area immediately south of the Swiss border, known as the Valtellina, was controlled by Austria but was claimed by the kingdom of Sardinia. The Italian patriot Garibaldi was stirring up nationalistic fervour, moving around the various city-states now comprising Italy. As a result, Austria enforced a trade ban and many of the Swiss who had been working in Lombardy and Venice were forced to return to their villages, joining the ranks of the unemployed. And even though the Val Poschiavo was safely ensconced in Switzerland, many young men of military age had a well-founded fear of conscription and were susceptible to enticements for emigration.

Opportunistic English, Dutch and German shipping agents based in Locarno visited the southern valleys offering competitive inducements for travel to North or South America and Australia. Most emigrants were keen to acquire land and establish themselves as farmers in the new lands overseas. Many were also aware of the stories of the men from Ticino who had become rich through finding gold in Australia. Emigration became a popular option for the unemployed and land-less Poschiavini in the 1850s. Groups of young men, dubbed 'caravans', were frequently farewelled from the town square in Poschiavo to travel north to ports such as Hamburg, Rotterdam and Liverpool. These occasions were replete with tears, vows to return and promises of remittances of the bounty reaped in unknown lands on the other side of the earth to the bereft families left behind.

The Mazzucchelli household was not a happy one at this time. Finances were stretched to the limit. Giuseppe's father, Antonio, earned little enough as a stonemason but as the family's fortunes declined, he spent more of his time and meagre earnings in the tavern. The more his mother, Maria, nagged on this matter, the more Antonio sought refuge in wine and the company of the more dissolute men of the village.

The marriage between Antonio and Maria started as a pure love match. The young Antonio, tall and handsome, arrived in Poschiavo from what was soon to become northern Italy and was much admired by the young women. He left his home town of Cortenedolo to escape involvement in the constant and seemingly pointless wars that beset the region at that time. It seemed to him everyone in the region he came from was obsessed with fighting, from domestic squabbles, neighbourhood rivalries, to the power struggles of the nobility. The latter frequently involved conscription and he was keen to avoid that. Switzerland was attractive because it seemed a more peaceful and orderly place in which to live. He secured work in Poschiavo as a stonemason but he found his celebrity status, as a visitor from outside the valley, a significant distraction. He was tall, with an upright bearing, high square shoulders, fine facial features and blue eyes, in contrast with the typically squat stature of the menfolk of Poschiavio. He enjoyed the adulation of the women and revelled especially on Sundays, when the citizenry dressed in their best clothes and, after attending either the Roman Catholic or Evangelical churches, spent the rest of the day parading around the town and chatting in cafes and taverns.

Maria had been one of the town beauties captivated by Antonio, who swept her off her feet, despite the antagonism of her family. Maria's family were traditionally well-to-do professional people, lawyers and doctors and felt Antonio, a mere stonemason, was not good enough for their daughter. However, she overcame their opposition and the newly-wed couple settled into a humble cottage in the village of Prada, a little more than one mile to the south of Poschiavo. They were united in their determination to do well and wanted to demonstrate to Maria's family that their opposition to the marriage was mistaken. However, things soon soured. Antonio's work was slow and poorly paid. Maria was constantly pregnant and looking after a succession of sickly babies. Of the first six children born to Maria, five of them female, only one, a girl, survived childhood. Death seemed to be ever present in the household. By the time Matteo was born, Antonio was starting to become embittered by the lack of robust offspring and the lack of sons, so important to a proud Italian man.

Maria's parents sought early in the marriage to alleviate the poverty of the couple with gifts of food and household goods. This injured Antonio's pride and he forbade Maria to accept their generosity. Arguments arose from this and soon Maria's parents were no longer welcome in the household. Maria maintained contact with her family in a furtive way, with visits to Poschiavo during the day while Antonio was at work. He was oblivious to the many meals he ate that were cooked with ingredients supplied by Maria's family. The children were sworn to secrecy about this deception.

The birth of three boys in succession; Matteo in 1837; Pietro in 1839 and Giuseppe in 1842, briefly revived Antonio's sense of equilibrium. However, the spectre of infant death returned when Pietro died, only twelve months old, and one of the three girls born after Giuseppe failed to reach puberty. From an early age, it was understood Matteo would work with his father and he left school early to do so. He was a solidly built lad with average intellect, a cheerful disposition and a willingness to work hard. Initially he welcomed the opportunity to learn his father's trade and they worked well together. Matteo's presence seemed to brighten any occasion, whether at work or leisure with the family or his friends. Once Matteo achieved competence as a stonemason, however, Antonio's attitude underwent a change. He seemed to feel he no longer needed to work so hard. He began to set Matteo menial tasks and would disappear for hours at a time. Matteo resented having to do the donkey work, made worse by being excluded from the more satisfying finishing touches on their constructions. He suspected Antonio was making more and more visits to the tavern during the working week, while he did most of the hard physical work. To top all this off, Antonio was reluctant to pay Matteo a fair wage.

Matteo was popular among the young people in Poschiavo and spent most Sundays socialising. He became aware many of his young friends were planning to emigrate to Australia. Matteo knew more than most about gold in Victoria from his discussions with Giuseppe and became determined to do likewise.

Giuseppe showed aptitude in his studies and his teachers hoped he might aspire to a profession. Antonio was adamant he should leave school and seek work as a labourer to help support the family. Maria wanted to seek financial support from her family to allow Giuseppe to continue his studies, but Antonio's pride led him to rail against this course. Maria confided in the parish priest, who schemed to keep Giuseppe at school and ultimately enter the church, a career which had no appeal for Giuseppe. Many an argument flared up over Matteo's shortcomings as an apprentice and Giuseppe's future career and on most occasions, ended with the slamming of the cottage door as Antonio stormed off to drown his sorrows at the tavern. Most of the arguing was between Antonio and Maria but as he grew more determined, Matteo joined in, declaring his intention to emigrate to Victoria. This enraged Antonio, who believed a son was obliged to work at whatever task his father found suitable. However, true to his word, in the autumn of 1858, Matteo packed his few belongings and set off for Liverpool with a large caravan of young men from Poschiavo. From there, he sailed in the *Scottish Chief* to Melbourne.

From the moment of Matteo's departure, the pressure on Giuseppe increased. Antonio expected him to become his apprentice in place of Matteo. Being aware of Antonio's slack work habits and bad temper, Giuseppe could see nothing ahead but doing the donkey work for his father or a life of celibacy as a priest. He felt aggrieved, it was he who had developed the knowledge and skills needed to fossick for gold and learned about the great goldrush in Victoria. Now his brother was en route to Melbourne and he was the object of a tug of war between his parents. He resolved to keep a low profile and await his opportunity to follow Matteo to the Victorian Goldfields.

From the time Giuseppe leaves with his caravan, travelling overland to Rotterdam, his port of departure, he adopts the Germanic spelling of his Christian name, Joseph, as written on his emigration certificate because it is the same in English. He opted for a small sailing ship mainly because it is cheaper. Most ships travelling between Europe and Australia combine sail and steam, for which higher fares are charged. Joseph's finances do not allow such luxuries. In any case, Matteo had described the long trip to Australia on board the *Scottish Chief* as a most unpleasant experience.

Some 22 emigrants from Poschiavo were part of a total of 225 passengers on the *Scottish Chief*, mostly British and Irish, on a journey that lasted 92 days. The Poschiavini felt themselves to be victims of discrimination throughout the voyage by the other passengers and crew alike, who disparaged them as 'the Italians.' They complained to the crew they were not getting their rightful share of the food on offer. Exasperation grew to such a level that at one stage a bewildered passenger was threatened with a knife. Later in the journey, when supplies of drinking water were running low, there were accusations the Italians had stolen from other passengers. In general, there was an atmosphere of mutual suspicion between the Poschiavini on one hand and the crew and passengers on the other, exacerbated by the cramped conditions on board and length of the voyage. Although much of the friction was no doubt due to misunderstandings arising from language difficulties, Joseph feels it best to avoid an English-dominated ship.

The tiny sailing ship *Schoonderloo,* departs from Rotterdam in mid-November 1859 with Joseph amongst the 23 passengers on board, mostly Poschiavini. After stopping for provisions at the Canary Islands, the ship continues to Melbourne, arriving in early March 1860 without making further landfall. It follows the shortest, great circle route, heading initially toward the eastern tip of South America, then turning eastwards between the 40th and 50th parallels of latitude.

Confinement and repetition are the best way to describe Joseph's sea voyage. The living quarters below decks are cramped. The deck space on the 480 ton vessel is restricted, limited further by cargo and the sheep, cows and chickens supplying fresh food for the long journey. Joseph takes every opportunity for exercise he can, but the deck is crowded in good weather and in bad weather he can only last short periods in the open air. The weather, for the first part of the journey, is dismally cold and wet. Joseph spends long hours in the cramped conditions below deck squinting in the dim light at the English language book he acquired before leaving Poschiavo.

Three days out from Las Palmas, the wind stops blowing and the sails hang lifeless. The *Schoonderloo* is becalmed under a blazing tropical sun. The sea is as smooth as a lake. Smoother still. It is glassy. Despite the stifling heat, most passengers remain below deck to avoid the scorching sun. The hours drag by. When the sun eventually sets, Joseph and some other passengers ascend to the deck. As night falls, it is still windless and warm. The sea is calm and a mesmerising phosphorescent green colour. The first stars appear, signalling the start of the nightly spectacle that has enthralled Joseph from his earliest times in the Bernina Pass. According to his reading of the familiar constellations, the boat is drifting aimlessly in the tropical waters. Joseph stays up on deck until he judges it to be cool enough to sleep and goes below.

The next morning, the windless calm continues. The heat returns under a relentless sun and most take shelter below deck. Joseph remains on deck with a few friends from Poschiavo when they see a curious smudge on the northern horizon. After watching it for ten minutes or so the smudge becomes a large steamship coming up astern, belching black smoke from its twin funnels. They shout and point it out to a crew member. A cluster of crew and excited passengers quickly grows.

'It looks like the *Great Britain*,' offers a crewman. He explains the *Great Britain* was regarded as the most innovative ship in the world at the time of its launch in 1845. It is more than 328 feet long and weighs 3,500 tons, seven times the size of the *Schoonderloo*. It includes all the latest developments, steel construction with watertight bulkheads, powered by steam with screw propulsion as well as sail. After initially operating as a luxury steamer-sailing ship between Liverpool and New York, it was reconfigured in the 1850s and became the fastest vessel on the England-Australia route, taking 700 passengers per voyage. The emphasis changed from steam to sail power to compensate for the lack of bunkering opportunities on the Australia route.

'That's where steam has the advantage,' says the informative crewman. 'While we wait for the wind to blow, they fire up their steam engine and keep going.'

When it overtakes the *Schoonderloo*, it passes within 50 yards, so the crew and passengers on both ships wave and shout greetings across the waves. By the time the *Schoonderloo* arrives in Melbourne, the *Great Britain* is already on its return voyage.

The wind picks up later that day, enabling them to continue their southwards trajectory. When they reach the 'Roaring Forties,' bitterly cold westerly winds and rough seas again restrict the time the passengers want to spend on deck. Repetition. The days pass in a blur. Sleep, eat, time on deck, time in cabin, eat, time on deck, time in cabin, eat, sleep. Although he remains on cordial terms with all on board throughout the voyage, Joseph is happy to keep to himself, with his dreams of finding gold in a new land.

Early one morning, Joseph is lying in his bunk thinking the pitching and rolling of the *Schoonderloo* in the southern Indian Ocean and then Bass Strait will never end, when the motion of the ship suddenly changes, now more of a slewing side-to-side. He rushes out of the cabin, scrambles up the ladder and reaching the deck with his heart bursting, catches sight of land to both port and starboard. The ship is passing through 'The Rip' at the mouth of Port Phillip Bay. Joseph rushes from one side of the ship to the other.

His first impression of his new home is the flatness of the land but his excitement is undiminished. To a young man from the mountains of Europe, this is new! The currents suddenly release their grip on the ship and for the first time in four weeks it is steadily sailing on the calm waters of the bay, under a blue, cloudless sky with a fresh south-west breeze astern. The waters of the bay sparkle under brilliant sunshine and Joseph inhales deeply of the sweet-smelling air. The land recedes as they sail into the bay. Nearing Melbourne, the shore draws closer and he can see more of his destination. Docking at Hobsons Bay, the skyline is a forest of masts and rigging from scores of ships bringing gold-seekers and machinery from Britain, Europe, North America, Africa and Asia. The docks are a confused, noisy hive of activity as incoming cargos of humans, livestock and sundry other goods are replaced by bales of wool and lumber heading back overseas. Joseph steps ashore in the early afternoon, eager to be on firm land after his long sea journey, only to find the dock rising and falling under his feet to the same rhythm as the ship's motion. Intending to waste no time before heading west through Ballarat to Pleasant Creek, he will need to recover his 'land-legs' first. Deciding it is too late to set off westwards, he sets out to explore Melbourne.

Joseph is surprised to be able to travel by train over the 10 miles from Hobsons Bay to the city. The train travels past a motley assemblage of warehouses, lumber yards and flimsy timber and corrugated iron dwellings, interspersed with swampy and marshy ground bordering a muddy river, but he's pleasantly surprised as the train approaches the outskirts of the city. Melbourne in 1860 has been in existence only some 25 years and is already showing signs of prosperity and permanence, largely a result of nine years of spectacular returns from gold mining. Joseph leaves his bag at a lodging place and spends the rest of the afternoon and early evening exploring the city on foot. Collins Street presents an orderly array of two and three-storey buildings on both sides of the wide street, bustling with commerce. The more substantial buildings look quite new. Many are constructed of 'bluestone,' a dark basalt Joseph will see in abundance on his way to Ballarat. He walks along the banks of the Yarra River, watching a paddlesteamer ferry pleasure-seekers between the city and Richmond. His walking dispels the aftermath of his sea voyage and he feels ready to tackle the long walk to Pleasant Creek via Ballarat. After a satisfying meal, he settles for the night, determined to make an early start the next morning.

2

Ballarat - Victoria, 1860

The next morning, Joseph is quickly on the road leading to Pleasant Creek, where his brother Matteo has settled. Deciding he will walk the first 68 miles to Ballarat, all the better to take in his new surroundings but also to preserve his dwindling supply of cash and regain his fitness after the long sea journey. Joseph is eager to explore Ballarat, the legendary city 'built on gold,' the existence of which he had first learned about from the Reverend Ernest Brenton. Matteo is not expecting him and he thinks he might linger a few days in such a famous place, even longer, if he can somehow manage to get work.

It is a fine, sunny morning as he heads west. With the sun behind him, everything sparkles. At first he travels through farmlands on a plateau cut at intervals by gullies. The land is only partly cleared and stands of eucalyptus trees rise from the straw-coloured stubble from last summer's harvest. He absorbs rather than consciously notes the flatness of the landscape, the immensity of the blue, cloudless sky and the grey-green foliage of the unfamiliar eucalypt trees. Flocks of colourful birds wheel overhead and fossick for grain amongst the stubble. He walks to a constant background of birdsong, carolling magpies, squawking cockatoos and lorikeets, chirps, tweets and whistles. On several occasions, he is momentarily startled by the raucous chattering of kookaburras in nearby trees. What a strange and cacophonous noise to come from such a handsome bird!

As the road winds down into the gullies and back up to the plateau he recognises the 'bluestone' volcanic rock, sometimes as a thin, flat layer forming a lip at the margins or at times, in more substantial masses clinging to the slopes of the gullies. He had seen dry-stone walls, made of this rock, marking out the farms earlier and of course, he recalled its use in many of the fine buildings he had seen in Melbourne. Cattle and sheep graze on the lush green grass in the gullies.

It is not long before the road takes him beyond the farms and into uncleared Australian bush. Walls of vegetation enclose the road on both sides but a layer of dust from the dry, pot-holed road hides the sheen of the leaves. The plateau gives way to more undulating terrain. He passes isolated, low hills dotting the landscape, unaware these are extinct or quiescent volcanoes, responsible for outpourings of the 'bluestone' lava thousands of years ago. He is not yet able to 'read' the rocks or topography of this very different landscape.

The road is reassuringly busy with traffic. He frequently comes across coaches, bullock wagons, buggies, single or groups of horsemen, raising clouds of dust as they pass. There are many pedestrians like himself, travelling in both directions. Most of the pedestrians acknowledge him with a wave and a 'Good Day' as he approaches and he quickly adapts to the courtesy himself. Later in the morning he finds a group of people peering at something in the bush at the side of the road. He duly stops to see what they are looking at.

A helpful person points, 'We're just looking at a colony of koalas.'

Joseph cannot believe his eyes. Koalas! He had no idea such an appealing animal existed. He lingers for a long time after the group of bystanders disperses.

Moving on, he comes across sheep, in small mobs, seemingly running wild. He passes through small settlements with a cluster of houses, a tavern, a shop and livery stables. Wood and corrugated iron are the main building materials but some clearly older houses are constructed of rough-hewn slabs of timber. He sees small groups of dark-skinned people, men, women and children, wearing an assortment of European clothing and animal skins. Reverend Brenton had not told him or didn't know about the indigenous people of Australia. The indigenous people Joseph sees look forlorn and separated from the bustling activity around them. At midday, he stops at a tavern to buy food. The premises reek of boiled mutton and cabbage but he finds the thick soup and bread offered is delicious and filling. On enquiring about the sheep, he is told they belong to wealthy 'squatters' who lease huge tracts of land, known as stations or runs. The biggest stations run many tens of thousands of sheep. Shepherds, who operate from a series of far-flung huts dotted around the stations, are supposed to keep an eye on the sheep. Joseph is not surprised to learn that shepherds had found the gold that started many gold rushes, recalling his own observations in the Bernina Pass.

It isn't long after resuming his journey, during a momentary lull in the traffic, that he sees a pair of kangaroos eating grass at the edge of the road. As he approaches, they prop on their hind legs and stare at him before turning and bouncing off into the bush. They are big creatures and he can hear their thudding retreat well after they disappear from view. Late in the afternoon of his first day on the road, a stiff breeze begins to blow and a bank of grey cloud advances from the south. The rustle of leaves in the treetops grows to a menacing roar. He picks up his pace and manages to reach a settlement just as it starts to rain. As he settles for the night he is happy with his progress and what he has experienced in his new country. He has been bothered by over-friendly flies and covered in dust from the road but his overall feeling is one of wonder at the freshness of the country and the friendliness of the people he has met.

Over the next few days the weather is changeable, often several times in a day but some part of every day is beautiful. He enjoys the following days even more. After the overnight rain, the vegetation looks fresh and green. The distinctive tang of the eucalyptus trees seems enhanced by the rain. Muddy puddles now occupy the wheel ruts, in place of the powdery dust, which he found suffocating at times in the previous day. The road crosses several streams, barely flowing after a long dry summer, before descending into a pleasant, cultivated valley. He comes to the small settlement of Bacchus Marsh, where he pauses for a hearty lunch. In the afternoon of his third day, he breasts a low hill and views what he later learns is Ballarat Flat. To the western and southern horizons lies an expanse completely cleared of trees. A swathe of hummocky, disturbed ground arcs southward in sinuous fashion, following the lowest parts of a shallow valley. Within this area, innumerable mounds of yellow-brown clay, soil and dark rock testify to past efforts to dig over and sift the earth for its golden content. There is little sign of human activity, although here and there he can see canvas tents. He turns off the main road to Ballarat to a side-track, descending the slope and leading through a maze of pits and shafts surrounded by piles of clay and white quartz. Dark basalt rock is visible on the dumps where lava had covered the gold-bearing alluvium. It is easy to see where the trees have gone. Timber posts mark out the mining leases. More tree trunks and limbs are used as tripods, headframes and windlasses, used to hoist the ore and waste rock from the shafts, which themselves are lined with logs. Horse-drawn whims for hoisting ore from the deeper shafts are also mostly constructed of bush timber.

Eventually, he comes upon the collection of corrugated iron and canvas buildings that comprise the township of Ballarat East. Here he locates a suitable cheap lodging place where he deposits his belongings and rests overnight before heading back out among the diggings for a closer inspection.

The next day, Joseph wanders along the dusty tracks which connect the various alluvial workings. To many, the surroundings would be repugnant but to Joseph, this is the reality he has long dreamed about. All the box and ironbark trees, even wattles, were cut down and redeployed in support of mining gold. Entire stream systems were dug over and processed through sluices and pans to recover gold, leaving a series of interconnected puddles and pools amongst hummocks of dug-over sand and clay. Grasses, shrubs and even tree saplings are beginning to re-populate the soil in inactive areas. Sinuous lines of pits and shafts signify where the stream systems were raided for the gold they contain. To start with, the diggings were shallow, harvesting the gold from the present-day streams. Enterprising diggers soon found richer pickings could be obtained from deeper channels carved out by ancestral streams thousands or more years ago. These 'deep leads' followed the general trend of the present streams. The vastness of the area worked is testament to the wide spread of gold and the effort spent by many diggers in seeking it. Most of the workings are deserted, the easy gold having run out after the first few years. Small parties of men are still working the alluvium but the pickings are lean, having already been worked more than once before.

Joseph is wandering near the famous Canadian Lead, when a cheerful voice greets him, 'You interested in some work, young fellow?'

The speaker is a tall rangy fellow, stripped to the waist and standing by a windlass atop a shaft dump in the midst of the workings. He is tanned and muscular, with a very athletic build, a big-boned, friendly face, unruly, wavy hair and a fetching grin.

'I'm trying to work this lease on my own and I could do with some help from a strong lad like you. I'll pay you the same wage as Ballarat United and 10 per cent of the gold we mine.'

It is just the sort of offer Joseph had hoped for. He realises he knows nothing of the man making the offer or the work he was likely to have to do but is reassured by the man's engaging and friendly demeanour. He finds his prospective employer is one Jake Francis, 30 years of age, who has taken on a lease, the Lady Beatrice, with a history of good gold production. Apparently, it had been abandoned by its previous owners because the gold had run out. Jake is confident more gold is there for the taking, although some hard work and risk is involved. He also has information to suggest plenty of gold has been left in the adjacent leases and with a little hard work they could both make a tidy sum. He intimates if all goes well, Joseph could become an equal partner in the enterprise. To Joseph, it seems to be just the opportunity he has come all the way from Switzerland to grasp. He can scarcely believe his luck.

The first step is an inspection of the shaft and underground workings. Jake leads the way down a rickety timber ladder hanging from the side of the shaft.

The daylight dims as they descend and by the time they reach the bottom, about sixty feet deep, they are in total darkness, apart from the pinprick of glaring white at the top of the shaft. Jake lights a candle and as Joseph's eyes become accustomed to the dark he takes in the scene, a bell-shaped chamber some twelve feet in diameter and six feet high, lined by an irregular patchwork of timber. In the gaps between the logs and saplings, damp clay is visible everywhere, oozing water. In fact, they are standing in water several inches deep, which is draining into a sump, about three feet square, which Jake tells him must be emptied every day before mining can commence. Most of the water appears to be seeping from the lowermost level. Jake points out the material behind the timbers has changed to a gritty sand with occasional pebbles of rounded quartz. According to Jake, this is the sediment from the bed of an ancient stream that contains particles of gold.

Two tunnels or 'drives' lead off in opposite directions from the chamber, each about three feet square, where the earlier miners excavated the sandy 'wash'. This material was hoisted to the surface and its gold extracted by sluicing and panning. The residue forms the mound surrounding the shaft at the surface. The drives only lead six or ten feet beyond the chamber, having collapsed after the initial gold had been extracted. Jake's strategy is to block off the existing drives with waste rock from the surface dumps, reinforce the openings with new timber supports, then explore a second wash zone exposed behind the timbering, which he suspects represents a tributary stream channel. Once this material is mined, he plans to tunnel through the wash at right angles to the known stream direction, to prospect for parallel stream courses, which he reckons had been located on an adjacent lease.

Joseph settles into the routine of mining alluvial gold from the buried river channel or 'deep lead' very quickly.

They spend the first hour each morning de-watering the shaft, taking turns, with one down the shaft filling the bucket or 'kibble' from the sump at the bottom and the other working the windlass at the top. The water from the shaft is emptied into wooden barrels at the base of the shaft dump, to be used later for washing the sand they mine to extract any gold. Each returning kibble is loaded with rocks and timber to be used during the day's work. Once the water is lifted and the materials lowered, they work together for several hours. The routine involves the setting of timber braces against the walls and over the top of the drive. Rocks plug the gaps between the timbers on the walls and where needed on the backs. Once the timber supports are in place, the drive is extended cautiously ahead of the timbering, three feet at a time. The clay overburden is first excavated by pick and shovel, exposing the gold-bearing quartz sand at the base which is carefully packed in sacks for later washing and recovery of any gold present. Jake then climbs the ladder to the surface and operates the windlass, whilst Joseph loads first the sacks of wash material, then any of the clay overburden that cannot be stored underground in the disused drives.

Jake insists on personally washing and recovering the gold. This is already in progress when Joseph climbs the ladder to the surface. He watches the process with anticipation, as the sacks of wash are progressively emptied into a large flat dish and agitated with water, finishing with a small 'tail' of glittering gold particles. These are carefully washed into a glass jar which Jake keeps in his pocket. Sometimes the 'tail' contains slugs of gold up to the size of a pea, a cause for jubilation. The amount of gold in each sack varies. Sacks with nil or poor yields signify a change in direction of the 'pay zone' which determines the next mining cut, the object being to always follow the rich 'leader.'

Jake seems as good as his word. Every Friday, Jake sells the accumulated gold to the local gold-buyer and pays Joseph his wages and what he believes is 10 per cent of the proceeds of their mining venture. Joseph soon finds himself attaining an unaccustomed affluence. He buys a tent and erects it next to Jake's on the nearest dry, undisturbed ground to the Lady Beatrice. They eat a simple breakfast and lunch together at the diggings and a hearty meal at night at one or other of the Ballarat taverns. At their evening meals, Jake adopts a serious, confiding tone, sharing with Joseph his ambitions for the Lady Beatrice. The gist of his message is that a fortune is there to be won. All they need to do is stick to their plans, work hard and soon they will reap the rewards. Those rewards will open a plethora of possibilities in this new land of opportunity: owning a shop, a hotel, a farm. Joseph could even return to Switzerland with enough wealth to set himself up for life. Joseph listens to all this with a mixture of scepticism and wonder.

On Fridays they are often joined at dinner by friends of Jake and the mood is different, more celebratory. These occasions tend to become rowdy with much drinking and chatter. Joseph is more an observer than a participant but he is glad to be included in such boisterous good company. He is somewhat mystified by the banter which ricochets around the table. Jake and his friends speak too fast for him to be able to translate and use a kind of code he does not yet understand. Occasionally, he suspects he is the subject of discussion, although no-one attempts to explain what is being said. Joseph is unable to match Jake and his friends in alcohol consumption and often finds it hard to stay awake when the drinking and yarning goes on too long. Sometimes, the festivities reach a point where the group decides to go on to places of bawdy entertainment. He usually excuses himself, but as he becomes more familiar with the routine, he finds no-one notices or objects when he leaves the group and wanders back to his tent. Sometimes he is woken by Jake, noisily returning to the camp in the middle of the night. On many Saturdays, Jake is slow to rise and when he does, suggests tasks Joseph can do without him. On Sundays, their habit is to go on an excursion into the bush to cut timber for mining supports. On these trips, Jake often shoots a kangaroo, the prime parts of which end up as a hearty stew which supplies their needs for several days.

As he settles into this routine of a digger's life, Joseph considers his adventure to be rewarding and exciting beyond his expectations. There is however some niggling unease. As the new drive progresses further from the shaft, he is aware of the ever-increasing danger of a collapse. At the same time, he realises Jake is spending less and less time with him at the face. There is always some reason why he needs to be at the surface, be it panning the wash, re-panning previous washings or reorganising the waste dumps away from the shaft. Joseph suspects Jake is spending increasing amounts of time loafing around with his friends while he slaves away down below, but he is not yet sufficiently confident to challenge his mentor.

At the start of a new day, after the sump is emptied and the water lifted to the surface, Joseph crawls along the drive with his candle and leather bucket to the work face. The drive has advanced four feet or so beyond the timber supports that provide a dubious assurance of protection from collapse. His pick and shovel are where he left them the previous day. He pauses before striking at the face with his pick. A faint sound breaks the silence. It grows in intensity, a creaking and a cracking. He realises with alarm the ground is 'talking.' A trickle of water appears in the face and in a few seconds begins to swell. He instinctively pulls back towards the shaft but not quickly enough. There is a loud 'crack' as support timbers snap, then a roar of falling earth. A slurry of mud is cascading over him. He consciously lifts his torso, sucks in a deep breath and holds it. The noise goes on for a long time and he fears he will be buried. Eventually it abates and the only sound he can hear is dripping water in the total darkness. He exhales and begins breathing the now dusty air. He is still alive but can he get out?

He feels around for his candle. It is nowhere to be found. In total darkness, Joseph moves back towards the shaft but almost immediately comes up against a mound of mud mixed with rock and broken timber, blocking the drive. He carefully climbs to the top of the debris, seeking an opening he can crawl through. He is unable to find an escape route.

He tries shouting, 'Help!' Silence. 'Help!' again. Silence. Joseph realises the gravity of his situation but to his surprise, feels calm. He ponders why Jake has not come to his aid. Surely he would have heard or seen something. Even if Jake hadn't realised there had been an accident, he would surely come down looking for him when he doesn't signal that he has ore to hoist to the surface. He feels he must wait longer for help to arrive and not risk another collapse by precipitate attempts to free himself.

After what seems an eternity, he hears a call but it isn't Jake. He recognizes the deep voice of Ed from the party working an adjacent lease but can't see him. He calls back, 'I'm not hurt but I can't get out.' A light appears from an unexpected direction, several feet to the left of where the drive used to be.

Ed says, 'It seems the roof has come in on your drive but there is an opening to the right. I don't trust it without some timber support. It could come down again. I'll go for more help. Just stay where you are, keep still and don't worry, I'll be back and we'll get you out.'

The wait feels like hours but is only a few minutes, Ed returns with his three mates, digging equipment and some timber to prop up the backs. They work quickly but cautiously, digging the muck out from the side of the mound, so they can open a route for Joseph to crawl out. Where possible, they place timber props to support the back before advancing again. It is only 15 feet to where Joseph crouches, but it takes two hours of hard digging and painstaking timbering work before Joseph is set free.

Back at the surface, having a cup of tea with his rescuers, Joseph learns a great deal about Jake, of which he was previously unaware.

'I've been worried about you. That Jake is a bad 'un.' Ed says. 'I suspected you were a bit green. I knew Jake would not hesitate to put someone like you to work at the face, not knowing the risks. I would have tipped you off if I'd had the chance. Did Jake tell you his previous partner died in a rock-fall in that mine?'

Joseph's face registers shock. He shakes his head in the negative.

'The Lady Beatrice has quite a reputation around Ballarat as a dangerous shaft,' continues Ed. 'I suspected Jake was exploiting your inexperience and had deliberately given you the most dangerous work. I questioned Jake about this a few days ago but was told to mind my own business.'

Ed neglects to add it was accompanied by an implied threat of violence.

'How did you know what had happened?' asks Joseph.

'That was easy, says Ed. 'I heard a loud 'whumphhh' and turned to see a puff of dust rising from the shaft. I knew what had happened when I saw Jake hurriedly pack his gear and head off in the direction of your camp. I was fairly certain I saw you arrive with Jake in the morning and suspected you were still down the shaft. When ground collapses underground, the displaced air generally makes a noise you can hear even at some distance and the plume of dust is a dead giveaway.'

Eating with his new friends that night, Joseph learns a lot about the business of prospecting and mining. Ed Clegsworth is typical of the diggers at Ballarat, toughened by the hard physical work of mining and eking out a living with a minimum of the comforts of civilisation. Like most diggers, his early life as a shepherd on one of the big sheep runs had been one of unremitting hardship. He saw the life of a digger as no worse than that from which he had come and an opportunity to achieve a more prosperous future. He is short and stocky in stature, with facial features almost completely obscured by a great bushy beard, tawny mane and shaggy eyebrows. He speaks with a deep monotone voice, which seems slightly muffled by his abundant facial hair, whilst fixing the listener with a steady, penetrating gaze. Ed can handle trouble if it arises but sees no point in looking for it if it can be avoided.

'There are many scoundrels and some ruthless men on the diggings and if you get into an argument it can quickly become violent. The best policy is to choose your partners carefully and keep away from trouble if you can. There are plenty of good men amongst the diggers, people who work hard to support their families back home. You'll also find many talented men with fascinating stories.' Ed says.

'Like that professor chap from Poland or somewhere,' says Charlie, one of Ed's partners. 'He left a university post to come and fossick for gold in Ballarat.'

'Oh, you'll find all sorts of men here; bankers, doctors and a fair few scalliwags as well,' says Ed.

That evening, when Joseph returns to where Jake's tent had been, everything has been dismantled and removed. Jake is nowhere to be seen but at least he'd left Joseph's tent and belongings. Joseph decides to spend the night in Patroni's boarding house to ponder his next move.

3

Stawell - Victoria, 1860 to 1863

Two months after his arrival in Ballarat, Joseph decides it is time to resume his intended journey to Pleasant Creek and reunite with his brother Matteo. At the time of his arrival, the settlement at Pleasant Creek is in transition to the town of Stawell. The alluvial rush, which had started in 1856, some three years after the initial discovery of gold in Pleasant Creek, is essentially over. The focus of activity is now progressively transferring to mining gold from quartz veins on the slopes of the Big Hill, some two miles to the east.

In 1853, William McLachlan, a Scottish shepherd, had washed a few ounces of gold from Pleasant Creek close to his slab hut, which was an outstation of Allanvale, one of the early sheep runs in the Wimmera District. Although McLachlan shared his knowledge readily with others in the district, there was no substantial activity in the area until three years later, when richer gold was found to occur in the deeper alluvial deposits below and flanking Pleasant Creek and other watercourses in the district. Thousands of eager diggers swarmed onto the field and spread out over an area of 20 or so square miles. Rich gold was also located at Deep Lead, some four miles to the northwest, with yields of up to 40 ounces of gold to the ton of alluvium excavated from pits from 3 feet to 103 feet deep. As news of the rich finds spread, diggers rushed to 'peg' adjacent ground and sink exploratory pits. Found through trial and error, the best yielding pits occurred in sinuous lines representing ancient, buried river channels. As these trends became apparent, additional pits were dug along the projected extensions, rapidly expanding the reach of the alluvial diggings. Many a digger earned what was at that time a fortune from a few days' work. Many more found nothing.

In September 1856, the population had swelled to some 8,000 at Pleasant Creek, 90 per cent of whom were males, the rest women and children. A small contingent of Chinese nationals was also there. Before the end of the year, it was estimated the population had grown to 30,000, spread between Pleasant Creek, Deep Lead and the quartz reefs on Big Hill. A ramshackle township had sprung up almost overnight. The main thoroughfare, Commercial Street, followed the meandering Pleasant Creek diggings over a distance of two miles. Most of the buildings were of a temporary nature, made up of combinations of timber, canvas and corrugated iron but within two years, some more substantial and imposing buildings were built. These included a treasury and warden's office, made of brick, a post office, police quarters, stables and lockup, which were of timber and iron. Most of the constructions along Commercial Street were shops and taverns but billiard saloons, dance halls, boxing booths, bowling and skittle alleys, gold-buyers, doctors, lawyers and, importantly, undertakers were also in evidence.

The population was highly mobile and mostly lived in tents at the diggings. As word of new finds arrived via bush telegraph, those not on 'good gold' would pack up their tents and belongings and set off to try their luck in the new location. For a few years, the population surged and waned at each of the main centres but by the time of Joseph's arrival in 1860, activity was dwindling in the alluvial fields and becoming ever more concentrated at the Quartz Reefs. The township of Stawell, proclaimed just two years before, was the name adopted for the growing settlement on the western flank of Big Hill, the centre of most of the quartz mining, although the informal names of

Pleasant Creek and Quartz Reefs were slow to drop from common usage. The gold here was in hard quartz veins which continued deep into the earth. The task of mining through hard rock and need for crushing equipment to liberate the gold required capital investment. Quartz reef mining became the province of syndicates and companies, rather than the individual or small groups of diggers, which were characteristic of the alluvial diggings. However, the mining companies employed diggers in increasing numbers as the quartz mines prospered and mining of alluvial gold dwindled. Work on the quartz mines was hard and dangerous and the wages meagre, so many diggers oscillated between working underground as miners and having another 'crack' at alluvial mining well into the 1870s.

Matteo is one of the latter. By the time Joseph arrives, he has been in Stawell for nearly two years. He has tried alluvial mining at both Pleasant Creek and Deep Lead with modest success but has, of necessity, joined the underground mining workforce. He is still a bachelor, working for wages at Big Hill and living in a boarding house. He had no warning of Joseph's arrival, so there is great jubilation when Joseph finds him at the mine gate at the end of his shift. It is late afternoon and they repair immediately to a hotel in Main Street Stawell, to eat, drink and tell their stories.

Matteo has plenty of tales of the excitement of the early rush in Pleasant Creek but they are mainly second-hand, his arrival on the field having also postdated the peak of the rush. However, rich alluvial patches are still found, albeit less frequently and he joined in the search with gusto. Initially, he had teamed up with another migrant from Poschiavo, Francesco Dorizzi, working old claims. Their first effort yielded just enough gold to keep themselves fed and after three months, they both decided to seek wages work as miners at Quartz Reefs to shore up their finances, before continuing their quest for riches. Their next foray into alluvial digging, at Deep Lead, was rewarded early when they hit a rich patch. They celebrated in traditional fashion, buying drinks for the bar at the nearest grog shanty. However, their golden streak died out and a month later they were again living from hand to mouth. Since then, Matteo had been working for wages for a syndicate sinking a shaft on Sloane's Reef, whilst Francesco had set out for Bendigo and was not heard of since.

When Joseph relates the story of his mishap in Ballarat, Matteo responds, 'They say you shouldn't let your hunger for gold override the need for caution. That's what I was told and you've already learned from experience. Overall, what do you make of Victoria?'

Joseph paused for thought before answering. 'I don't find the scenery or the eucalyptus trees very attractive but it all seems so new, almost untouched. There must be lots of opportunities to make a good life here.'

'It's different and it takes a while to grow on you, but you'll find it really is a beautiful country when you get used to it. It took me three months or so before I learned that, but I agree our opportunities here are unlimited, far better than Poschiavo.'

'Talking of Poschiavo, have you been able to send any money home?' asks Joseph.

'Not yet, but I've found out how to do it. I'm ready to send a few pounds within the next week,' says Matteo. 'And I'll make sure it goes to our mother, not the old man.'

'Don't be too hard on him.' Joseph said, 'I think your walking out on him had a big effect. He was working harder and drinking less when I left. I don't think he will be able to work as a stonemason very much longer. It's a young man's trade. I think our parents are hoping to be able to rent or purchase a small landholding so they can grow vegetables and have some livestock to supply their needs. I'd like to think we could help them do that.'

By the time Joseph had recounted his adventures since arriving in Melbourne it is late and the brothers go back and spend the night in Matteo's lodgings. Matteo advises Joseph to seek mining work at Quartz Reefs as soon as possible. When he is settled, they should join forces in prospecting on the weekends. The next day, Joseph finds work at the Scotchman's Quartz Reefs Mining Company and starts to learn about underground mining.

Joseph's first descent to the underground workings of the Scotchman's Reef is an unnerving experience. Two horses, harnessed to a whim, walk alternately clockwise and anti-clockwise, to raise and lower a heavy steel kibble to the workings at 100, 200 and 300 feet below the surface. Joseph stands with another three men in the kibble, holding onto the haul rope for support, as the party descends to the 300 feet level. The kibble sways and lurches on the way down and it is necessary for all occupants to push off the walls of the shaft with one hand to keep the kibble from snagging on the rough rock walls. Joseph learns it is not uncommon for a kibble to catch on a protruding rock or loose timber on the way down, tipping the occupants out, sometimes with fatal results. As they descend, the rocks roughly lining the shaft change in colour from a light brown to dark grey and water starts to trickle and drip. The light quickly diminishes as they go down and eventually becomes a bright pinprick far above them. On reaching the working level, the kibble stops and they climb out, finding themselves in a small room carved from the rock and lit by an oil lamp. The group leader, Arthur, tugs a rope at the side of the shaft, which rings a bell at the top and after a pause, the kibble departs, heading up to the surface.

The miners light candles, gather their tools and set off along a narrow tunnel. After 30 feet or so they come to a point where the tunnel branches into two, both running perpendicular to what he learns is the 'cross-cut.' These tunnels or 'drives' follow the quartz vein containing the gold. At first, the roof of the drive is completely lined by timber, supported by thick timber poles on either side of the drive. This is where the vein has already been mined above the level of the drive. Going further along the right hand drive, the timbering ends and the 'backs' consist of jagged rock. Joseph can see the quartz vein, white in colour, contrasting strongly with the dark grey shale, despite a coating of grime. The quartz vein runs more or less along the middle of the backs. It does not run straight but whichever way it turns, the drive follows it. At this point, the vein is only a matter of two to four inches wide, too thin to be payable but easily traceable. The mining crew continues in silence for what seems a great distance along the drive. The walls are coated with a thick layer of grey dirt. The floor is uneven and treacherous. Light rail lines are laid on sleepers, directly over a layer of loose rock and mud. Water trickles and seeps down the walls of the drive, adding to pools and rivulets working their way back to the shaft, where a sump requires constant pumping.

Joseph finds it difficult to find a firm footing and can barely keep up with his companions, while taking in the sights and sounds of this strange new environment. When they pause to make sure he is still with them, Joseph can clearly hear intermittent tapping noises, the sounds of working parties in other parts of the mine, transmitted through solid rock. They pass three more areas of timbering, where the vein has swelled to sufficient width to warrant mining Eventually, they come across what looks like a newly timbered area. This is where they start mining.

They climb up a ladder through a gap in the timber and find themselves standing on a pile of rock, mostly white quartz, looking up at the vein from which the rock was blasted. They set about drilling blast holes for the next charge of dynamite. This involves one man holding a steel rod with a hardened chisel tip up to the rockface while his partner hits the blunt end with a sledgehammer. With each blow, the holder is expected to rotate the steel ready for the next hammer strike. After a time, the holder and the striker swap jobs. In this painstaking way, a pattern of holes is drilled into the quartz reef which can be charged up with explosive and which, when detonated, will release several tons of gold-bearing quartz to be hoisted to the surface for processing.

It is dangerous work. The sledgehammer swings with frightening speed and force and the holder must hold not only the drill steel but more importantly, his nerve, lest the hammer miss and hit his hand or arm. Accidents are not uncommon in the semi-dark. Miners are hit by chips sent flying during drilling or rocks falling from the backs. Their lungs are damaged by inhaling rock dust when extracting the broken ore from the stopes, leading to many an early death from 'miner's lung.' later known as silicosis.

Joseph initially enjoys the new experience of working underground. He finds it hard to believe he is actually working in a gold mine. On many occasions, he sees rich seams of free gold in the quartz vein, either in the face or amongst the rock blasted free that forms the platform on which they work. His team gathers around to admire beautiful specimens of gold but although some might be tempted to pocket a rich piece, they remain loyal to their employers. He quickly forms a cooperative and trusting relationship with his workmates and relishes the Australian concept of mateship. At the same time, he learns the ropes of underground quartz mining and the ethos of extracting wealth from Mother Earth, even though very little is finding its way to his pocket. He also wonders how the gold he sees underground ends up in soil and streams when deposits like this are weathered and eroded at the surface.

Within a week, Joseph has his own room in a boarding house and begins to feel at home in Stawell. He spends most evenings with Matteo and they begin to plan their prospecting venture. They spend the next few weekends walking between Stawell, Pleasant Creek and Deep Lead, making observations and enquiries about vacant lease-holdings. One weekend, they hire horses and ride southward to the foot of the Grampians mountain range and have a picnic lunch by a mountain stream. This area has something of the appeal of the mountains of their homeland in Switzerland, even though there is no snow to be seen. The chilly freshness of the streams, clean-washed shingle and surrounding dense vegetation, although very different, conjure feelings of belonging. After lunch, they climb a sandstone spur on the north side of the range, inhaling the clean air and marvelling at the distance they can see over the gently undulating terrain to the north. The diggings at Pleasant Creek and the rapidly developing town of Stawell are the only signs of mankind's hand in the vast landscape dominated by stands of majestic eucalypt trees. Here and there are lakes and swampy areas along watercourses, marked by thickets of more dense vegetation. The brothers agree the land would be ideal for farming if only it could be wrested from the squatters, who control vast landholdings but are content to graze their sheep on the native grasses, without any attempt to work the land.

The biggest problem for Matteo and Joseph is deciding where to start prospecting for alluvial gold. As the initial alluvial rush at Pleasant Creek and Deep Lead, like Ballarat, is well and truly over, their search is largely conducted in ground already picked over by earlier diggers. They check the outskirts of the known areas for prospects that have been missed, taking samples of alluvium to the creek and checking for gold with a prospector's dish. They focus more on abandoned pits and shafts in the midst of known alluvial runs, where the earlier workers might not have been sufficiently thorough. Such prospects are sometimes very rewarding, given the nature of gold rushes. A digger will often abandon a lease without fully testing it when reports or rumours of a rich find elsewhere become known. A shallow pit surrounded by deeper shafts might indicate a prospect where good gold remains. They also test the spoil dumps around the shafts and pits. If they are lucky, they might find small slugs of gold lying in full view on old dumps, exposed by recent rain. Provided the ground is not covered by an existing mining lease, there is nothing to stop them picking up or 'specking' the odd piece of gold.

The brothers accumulate a small quantity of gold from their prospecting activity, washings from their gold-panning and specking. More importantly, they identify areas where they think they may make a find, although these patches are not always available. Other diggers are active in the area and there is competition for the best sites to explore. They keep a record of patches they would like to peg if the current owner relinquishes the lease. When they identify an available area they think is a prospect, they put in pegs to mark the corners and apply for a lease. This will start a period of hard work. It might consist of re-working the dumps, digging and transporting tons of material to water, where any remaining gold is to be extracted using a sluice or cradle. It might involve sinking a shaft to look for buried river gravels, which could contain gold in sand-sized grains or if they are lucky, pea-sized nuggets. As a result of their labours, they add to their stash of gold but never in amounts that make a significant difference to their lowly financial status. Nevertheless, the gold they gain from their prospecting, added to the wages they earn from their mining employment, puts them on a sound financial footing and they live well. They even send several small sums of money to the family back in Prada. And there is always the expectation or hope that their next prospecting endeavour will make their fortune.

The town of Stawell is growing apace. A commercial centre has developed on Main Street, which runs down from Big Hill towards Pleasant Creek. Many of the shopkeepers close their shops at Pleasant Creek and open more permanent premises on either side of Main Street. Substantial public buildings begin to take shape, a town hall, municipal offices, churches, and schools. There are plans for civic amenities. The town soon boasts several parks, a sportsground and a race-track. Life in Stawell is becoming civilized. In contrast to the early gold rush days, when men dominated the population, families are becoming established in the town. The female population is no longer limited to barmaids and prostitutes. Respectable and attractive young ladies are now noticeable around the town. This is not lost on the young single men, especially Matteo but also Joseph. They agree Stawell has much to offer and they would be content to settle and build their lives here.

Although Joseph's life in Stawell is dominated by work, underground mining for the Scotchman's Company during the week and fossicking for alluvial gold on the weekends, he habitually spends his evenings in town with Matteo and his friends. The working day at the mines starts and finishes early, allowing miners free time in the late afternoon and evening. Usually strolling through the town, they have a meal in a café or hotel, after which they might take a nightcap in one of the hotels, then go to their respective lodgings to sleep. An occasional game of billiards, a visit to a music hall or playhouse would break the monotony. Joseph is very much a passive participant in this group, enjoying the company of his brother and his brother's friends but rarely expressing an opinion or disclosing his thoughts. His naturally shy disposition, coupled with his limited English language, makes conversation difficult for him.

The pattern persists for the first year or so Joseph is in Stawell but is disrupted when Matteo takes a fancy to one Margaret Turner, an attractive girl some nine years his junior. Matteo's lifestyle quickly and dramatically changes. He is no longer available to spend evenings with Joseph and his friends and with increasing frequency, is missing at meal times as well. More importantly for Joseph, Matteo now finds it necessary to spend Sundays in town, rather than prospecting. It seems he must go to Mass at St Patrick's Church with the Turner family. He spends the rest of the day with Margaret, strolling through the town, at one of the parks or at home with the family.

Matteo feels guilty at the impact of his infatuation with Margaret on Joseph, particularly now Joseph is working twice as long as he is on their prospects. He suggests it is time Joseph should start taking Sundays off as well. He even gets Joseph to accompany him to church on two consecutive Sundays but Joseph, whilst happy for his brother's situation, is as unimpressed as he had been with church-going in Poschiavo. Immediately after the first mass he attends, Matteo insists they mingle with the congregation, which, as previously pointed out, includes several attractive single females. Matteo and Margaret introduce Joseph to two young ladies but he finds he has nothing to contribute to the conversation that ensues and feels distinctly uncomfortable.

After mass on the second Sunday, he heads off promptly to his lodgings to change into his working clothes and head for the diggings. As he is passing the Presbyterian Church in Main Street, his gaze is drawn to a rather tall and lean girl shepherding a group of Sunday School infants within the church grounds. He doesn't perceive her as a beauty and she is wearing a smock, a rather dowdy, shapeless affair, which does nothing to reveal her figure. But there is something about her movement and demeanour that makes her noticeable. She undoubtedly possesses a certain vivacity. Joseph doesn't think much more about it at the time but it seems amazing to him how often he begins to see her around the town. It seems every time he is walking through Stawell, she appears, crossing the road in front of him or standing chatting with friends outside the café where he often eats his evening meal. Joseph had also seen her on the previous Sunday walking with her family in the park, where he had gone to clear his head after his awkward meeting with Margaret's friends at St Patrick's and recollects her father had been a very stiff and formal-looking individual, while her mother was short and plump, seemingly with a scowling face. She appeared to have several younger siblings. He hadn't met her and wasn't sure he wanted to, considering she was obviously very religious and an adherent of an alien culture, a Protestant.

One evening when Matteo is eating with the Turner family, Joseph enters one of the new tea-rooms that has popped up in town for dessert and coffee. The waitress is none other than the girl who he is beginning to suspect is stalking him. She greets him warmly, takes his order and delivers it with efficiency and a certain charm. She looks more attractive in her uniform, consisting of a black full-length skirt and white bodice, than in her customary street clothes. They still have not met but now he knows where she works. Joseph is intrigued but doesn't feel the need to rush back to the tea-rooms.

A few days later, he is walking towards his boarding house late in the evening when he finds her walking beside him. She says a cheery 'Hello,' as if they were already friends and asks, 'Aren't you the man I served at the tea-rooms last week? I'm Ellen Greene and I'm on my way home after work. What's your name?'

Joseph is a bit taken aback by her familiarity but responds anyway. He has to spell out his surname for her and she immediately asks where he comes from. His answers bring forth a torrent of questions about Switzerland and what brought him to Victoria.

'I want to find some gold. It has been my aim for many years and why I came to Australia,' Joseph tells her.

'My father is a prospector. He used the gold he found to buy a farm. If you are successful at prospecting, what would you do?'

'I would like to become a farmer or own a shop.' Joseph responds and goes on to explain how he learned about Victoria's gold rush. They are still talking when they reach his lodging house but he finds he is enjoying the encounter and decides to keep walking with her. Eventually, she stops outside what he perceives is the Greene's cottage and she bids him goodnight. In doing so, she implies they should meet again soon and continue the conversation.

Ellen Greene is a revelation to Joseph. He has had little contact with females since coming to Australia and only engaged in small talk with the few he has met. Matteo's attempts to introduce him to the young ladies at St Patrick's Church left him struggling for words, so he felt socially inept and embarrassed but somehow he finds it easy and enjoyable to converse with Ellen. She doesn't stir romantic feelings, yet she is good company and seems to share a similar outlook to him.

After the first encounter, Joseph patronises Tippett's Tea Rooms almost daily and looks forward to the brief exchanges with Ellen. He still lacks the confidence to suggest meeting outside the formality of the tea rooms but Ellen cannily suggests he start coming for his supper half an hour before closing time so he can walk her home and chat with her. Walking home, he finds Ellen is a good talker. Initially, she does most of the talking, telling him all about her love of family, God, the Australian bush and how exciting it is to be in Victoria in general and Stawell in particular. In her view, life in Australia at this moment is full of boundless opportunity 'and we should make the most of it'. Joseph is surprised but compliant in the fact he seems included in her future ambitions. She tells him she has recently moved to Stawell from Beaufort, a small town he had been through en route between Ballarat and Stawell, where the family owns a farm. It transpires her father had success as a prospector at the Fiery Creek gold rush in 1854. As the gold rush subsided, Austin Greene used his earnings to purchase a parcel of land in the same area, which was re-named Beaufort. However, the returns from farming were insufficient to support his growing family, so they moved to rented accommodation in Stawell, where Austin is employed by one of the quartz mining companies. The farm at Beaufort was left in the care of a farm labourer.

'Our whole family goes back to Beaufort as often as we can to see how the farm is going. We have great fun, even though we work hard. I like to get my hands dirty with farm work. After the tea rooms it's like a holiday.'

Joseph says nothing, so Ellen continues, 'When we're in Stawell we usually spend Sunday morning at church and the afternoon in the park. I saw you there two weeks ago. Will I see you there next Sunday?'

'No. I will be working on my claim at Pleasant Creek.'

'Where is your claim? Perhaps I could come and see what you are doing. I may be able to help you. I like prospecting.'

Joseph gives her directions, little expecting she will come but sure enough, about three o'clock on the Sunday, she appears, carrying a basket containing four scones and jars of jam and cream. Joseph has been working at deepening the shaft and is ready for a break.

'Can you boil the billy for a cup of tea?' she asks.

'It'll only be black. I don't have any milk,' Joseph responds.

'That's all right. I'm not fussy. As long as we have something warm and wet to go with these scones.'

They sit down together on a log of wood. Little by little, she coaxes him into conversation, drawing from him details of his family and his life in Switzerland. The topic soon turns to prospecting.

'Isn't it wonderful to be able to earn money by prospecting for gold?' ventures Ellen.

'I haven't made any real money so far and I'm still learning and I'm still hopeful. I get excited by the thought that the next shovel-full of dirt might lead to a fortune.'

'Do you really want a fortune?'

'Not a fortune but enough to live well, perhaps set myself up in a business like farming, a shop or a tavern. I don't think I am greedy but I do believe we all need to do what we can to support ourselves and our family. If I was back in Switzerland, I would barely have enough to eat three meals a day, let alone buy clothes or go to the doctor when I'm sick and that would be my life until I die. Here, I earn enough to eat well, enjoy some pleasure and still send some money back to my family.'

'I agree with that,' said Ellen. 'And look at how prosperous gold mining has made Victoria. It's not just the successful diggers who have prospered. The local businesses that cater for the mining community, the transport industry, mining equipment manufacturers, the taverns, the government and so on. Anyway, it's time for you to get back to work. What can I do to help?'

Joseph ignores the question and climbs down the shaft, fills a bucket, climbs back out and hauls the dirt to the surface using a rope. He fills a dish and starts to pan for gold using water from a barrel.

Ellen says, 'Can I do that? My father taught me how to pan for gold.'

Joseph passes the pan to Ellen and watches while she expertly jiggles and rotates the pan, scraping the coarse and lighter material off, retaining the denser grains. When she is satisfied, she triumphantly shows Joseph the result, a tail of gold dust half an inch long.

'Well done!' says Joseph. 'I can see you have learned the art of panning well but what am I going to do if you take over the easiest job.'

'Oh, you can do the hard jobs, like digging more dirt and fetching more water.'

He laughs and they do indeed work this way for the rest of the afternoon, adding a few pennyweights of gold to Joseph's glass jar. Joseph is very tired but pleased with the result and glad to have Ellen's company. On the way home, they chat amiably. On parting, Ellen enquires, 'Can I come and work with you next Sunday? I'll bring you a nice lunch.'

Joseph readily agrees. Over the next few weeks, Ellen joins him at the prospect each Sunday at lunch time with a basket of delicacies, cold lamb chops, ham, bread, cheese, salads, fruit, biscuits, cake and milk for the tea. They usually walk off into the bush flanking the diggings, picking a nice shady, secluded spot. Ellen articulates her view that food is at its most enjoyable when consumed in the open air and makes an effort to make each Sunday lunch a celebratory picnic. Joseph has never eaten so well.

Over lunch they find themselves engaging in wide-ranging discussions, covering all the local topics of the day, progressing to the politics of the colonies, religion and their personal ambitions. Joseph starts the religious discussion with a question: 'What do you do at that Presbyterian Church on Sunday mornings?'

'I teach Sunday School. My father is the Superintendent of the Sunday School. I have been going to church all my life. Our family goes to an early service, then stays for Sunday School as teachers or pupils until eleven o'clock. Then I am free to come and join you.'

Joseph says, 'I was brought up as a Catholic but I don't go to church now. My mother wanted me to become a priest but I have a poor opinion of priests and the church. I grew up to believe the Catholic Church is the only true church. The Pope is infallible after all.'

'Oh, no! That's not so. The Pope is just a man. He might be a good man but he makes mistakes like all of us and your church is the Roman Catholic Church. There are other Catholic Churches such as the Eastern Orthodox, the Anglican, Lutheran and even the Presbyterian Churches.

Most of the mainstream Christian Churches regard themselves as Catholic in that they are universal and have maintained continuity from the original apostles.'

'Why do you think it is better to go to the Presbyterian Church instead of the Catholic Church?'

'Many reasons. For one thing, the whole service is in English, which everyone can understand, instead of Latin, which only the priests understand and I don't like the idea that priests cannot marry. I don't see how a man who has never married and had children can really understand the needs of ordinary people.'

Joseph asks, 'Why are there so many different Christian Churches?'

'I don't really know but I suppose different people have interpreted the Bible in different ways and grouped together to worship according to their different views. That's not a bad thing, anyone can find a church that makes them feel comfortable and meets their needs. But we all follow the teachings of Jesus and worship the same God. Our family goes to the Anglican Church in Beaufort but we prefer the Presbyterian Church in Stawell. My father thinks the Presbyterian minister is intelligent and stimulating.'

Joseph can see Ellen has ready answers for any questions he might have. She has clearly invested more effort into religious matters than he and is strongly committed to her beliefs. He would need good arguments to shift her opinions but he is not inclined to argue on this issue.

After starting as a self-acknowledged outsider, shy and withdrawn at that, Joseph soon finds he is bursting with opinions and eager to debate with her on any topic under the sun. Although they differ on many matters and never refrain from expressing their arguments with passion, they manage to keep a lid on their tempers and often reach compromises surprising each of them.

He soon finds her shapeless and drab clothing is also deceptive. Some weeks later, they are sitting side by side on the grassy bank of Pleasant Creek, under a shady willow, when he impulsively reaches out and draws her to him. She gives no hint of resistance and he trembles with excitement at the feel of her slim waist and the curve of her hips. They kiss briefly, then, sensing his change of mood, she wriggles free from his grasp and runs a few steps to the water's edge. Joseph lies back and shuts his eyes, wondering whether he has just ruined a precious relationship. The next thing he knows, an icy shower of water cascades over his head and shoulders. Momentarily shocked, he leaps to his feet, brushing the drops from his coarse woven jacket and his hair. He immediately sees she is not offended by his ardour. She is clearly in a playful mood.

'I had to do something to cool you off,' she laughs. 'You'd have a poor girl like me in trouble in no time at all.'

His anxiety evaporates. Two can play at this game. He lunges towards her, lowering his shoulder and lifts her off the ground like a fireman. She alternates between feigned indignation and laughter, punching his back none too gently, while he spins giddily around. His foot lands on some hard-packed but slippery mud on the sloping bank. He loses traction for a moment, makes several staggering efforts to regain balance, then collapses with a splash into the water. He is mortified as he sits up spluttering and festooned with green weed from the creek but Ellen is not in the least deflated. She heaves with mirth and holds out her arms to Joseph, to help her to her feet.

'I am so sorry,' he falters.

'Well, it's been a warm day and it would be a pity not to have had a dip,' she replies, flicking water from her dress.

'You cannot go back to your parents as wet as you are,' he says, picking green weed from his hair.

'Oh, stop worrying. Look, it's still early. Let's walk along the creek until we are away from the other people. We can dry our clothes in privacy and no one will know the difference.'

By the time they wend their way over mounds of worked dirt, through the eucalypt trees and scrubby wattles lining the banks of Pleasant Creek for a mile or so, they have left the sounds of Stawell well behind. He follows in her wake, gazing with admiration at her purposeful tread. He reflects that he is happy for her to take the lead and not just in this matter.

Reaching a small clearing by the side of the stream, she stops and looks around and satisfied they are sufficiently isolated, starts to unbutton the front of her dress. Joseph stands ogling as she coolly strips down to her cotton underclothes, seemingly unaware of his steadfast gaze. With graceful movements, she drapes the sodden grey dress over a low wattle bush so that it is in full sunlight. He takes in her usually hidden features, her slender but shapely legs and arms, the tiny waist, the swell of her hips and the perfect contour of her small breasts in silhouette through the white undergarments.

'Come on, stop staring. I'm just a girl,' she says, turning her attention to Joseph's sodden clothes. 'Get them off before you catch pneumonia,' reaching for his coat buttons.

He retreats a step, turns his back to her and removes his coat, shirt, boots and trousers. Feeling conspicuous and silly in his underdrawers, he hesitates near to where Ellen is stretching out on the sloping grass to sun herself, seemingly unaware of the tumult of emotion racing around in Joseph's mind.

'Come closer, you act as though you've never been near a girl before.'

She didn't know how near and how far from the truth was this remark. Joseph had lived in a ruthlessly male society ever since he had left his mother's and sisters' last embraces in Prada, two years before. Only once had he come into intimate contact with a female and it had been a most unsatisfactory and highly embarrassing experience. When he had been working in Ballarat, soon after his arrival in Australia, he had gone for a meal with Jake Francis and his rough mates after a relatively successful yield of gold from the Lady Beatrice. After they had all had rather too much to drink, a cry went up. 'Let's go to the brothel.' The whole group had gone to a brothel and one by one the men had paired up with one or other of the women in attendance and disappeared down the passage to the rooms at the back of the house. Joseph felt he should leave at this stage but was fascinated by the activity of this unfamiliar environment and found the partly dressed women not unattractive.

When his companions returned, they found Joseph sitting where they had left him, staring around with wide eyes. They quickly realised his lack of experience and insisted he should lose his virginity then and there. They called for a whip-around to cover the cost, called over an available woman and pushed the two off with the cash. Once the door was shut behind him, Joseph realised what was expected but still felt reluctant and awkward. Sensing his plight, the girl beckoned him to come and sit by her side on the bed. She asked his name, what he was doing in Ballarat and chatted amiably with him about events of the day.

He learned her name was Iris, that her mother had been brought out from Ireland on a convict ship and had succumbed to drink and died when Iris was only fourteen. It seemed to her that prostitution was the only avenue open to her but she hoped to earn enough to get a respectable job soon. She told him it was up to him but if he didn't want to have sex, that was all right but they should stay in the room long enough so his companions wouldn't be aware he hadn't taken advantage of their 'generosity.' It would also be a good idea for him to make some disparaging remarks about her as he left, which is what most of the men did to show their mates they were connoisseurs of performance in this field.

After some more small talk, she suggested it was time for him to go. As they rose, she drew him to her and kissed him fondly. As he felt the contours of her body against him, there was a stirring of passion and for a moment he thought he might like to complete the experience. However, she had already decided he was not to lose his virginity this night and propelled him back towards his friends, her demeanour suggesting boredom and indifference. He was more confused than ever at this and forgot his role as the dissatisfied customer but his friends were too weary and drunk to notice and the evening ended without his being called to account. He was to remember his encounter with Iris as a significant and enjoyable experience but one best kept to himself.

From that time until now, he has not had the urge or confidence to seek out female company. Now Ellen has seemingly sought him out, he feels the first stirrings of love, which he has hitherto bottled up. Looking at her as she lies with eyes closed on the grass in the bright sunlight, he realises she is indeed beautiful, not just in the physical sense but as a whole person. He bends over and lightly kisses her on the lips. Her eyes open and she smiles at him. She reaches upwards and draws him down on her and they lie embracing for a long moment.

He rolls onto his back, folds his hands behind his head and looks at the puffy clouds moving in from the west and thinks for the first time about a future shared with Ellen Greene. He realises with wonder that she has been one step ahead of him and has already committed herself to him. Ellen rolls over and cradles her head on his shoulder, her dark, wavy hair tickling his nose and cheek. He feels a wave of euphoria sweeping over him. He has experienced excitement, danger, success and almost every other emotion since he has come to Australia and now he realises how much he has been missing. He curls his arm around and gently squeezes her shoulder, feels her quiver slightly and together they drift off to a contented doze.

Later when they are making their way back to Stawell, he asks the question he strangely has not thought to ask before:

'How old are you?'

Joseph is rocked by her answer. Ellen is only 13. He is 21. Despite her slender figure, her mature attitude and confident conversation created the impression she is nearer his age. He previously thought of her only as an engaging companion, notwithstanding she is female. Now his thoughts have taken a more romantic turn, he realises the difference in their ages is a significant issue. He will have to think carefully before he presses his suit too strongly.

Joseph's world turned upside down. His thoughts revolve around the unexpected discovery that he is in love and the implications it brings. He will have to front up to Ellen's stern and forbidding father and ask for permission to marry his daughter. He is conscious he is a poor, uneducated immigrant, with a limited grasp of the English language and there is the question of religion. She is a Protestant and he a Catholic, albeit lapsed and he knows how the full force of the church establishment will insist the wedding take place and their children are brought up in the Roman Catholic Church. Lastly but importantly, Ellen is very young, in reality, too young for marriage. Although she seems much more mature than 13, can a girl this young be ready to make such a momentous decision? It seems to Joseph like an insoluble dilemma.

The following Sunday, he finds he is unable to concentrate on the claim he is working jointly with Matteo. Matteo, as usual, is spending the day with Margaret Turner. Ellen has gone to Beaufort with her family to check on the farm. Joseph is missing her and the scrumptious lunch she brings every Sunday. He walks back along Pleasant Creek to think about his future and finds himself wandering towards the wattle thicket where he had lain with Ellen while their clothes dried in the sun. The dense wattle scrub appears to climb up the bank of the stream in a smooth gradient, terminated by a stand of eucalypts at the upper margin of the valley. For no particular reason, he pushes his way deep into the midst of the wattles and finds, to his surprise, the ground initially slopes upwards but then descends again into a shallow depression, where the wattle trees appear to grow taller than those around them, giving the false appearance of a regular slope. He surmises, with some excitement, this depression might represent an oxbow or a disused section of Pleasant Creek. It seems to have escaped the notice of the early alluvial diggers because of the deceptive appearance of the wattle scrub. Joseph decides he will peg a claim and prospect the area himself on Sundays when Matteo is no longer available to work with him.

The following week he discusses his plans with Ellen, who not only agrees he is entitled to claim full ownership of the new prospect but also expresses her eagerness to work with him whenever she can. He then approaches Matteo with some trepidation to announce his intentions. To his relief, Matteo readily agrees it is time for them to terminate their joint efforts and go their separate ways. The claim they had been working was not yielding sufficient gold to justify their labour and Matteo himself is too busy courting Margaret to justify their partnership. He is planning to propose marriage. Joseph reflects on the irony that he had already had four sisters with the name Margaret, three of whom had died as infants and it seemed he was about to gain a fifth as a sister-in-law.

Joseph starts work on his new claim the following weekend. The first task is to retrieve his tools and other equipment from the old lease. He then cuts down the wattle trees growing in the depression. Around midday, Ellen arrives with a picnic lunch of bread, cheese, cold mutton and home-made chutney. They sit by the stream and eat with gusto. Joseph lights a fire and boils a billy to make tea, which always tastes so much better in the bush. After the meal, Joseph lies back and gestures to Ellen to do likewise, looking to repeat the embraces they had shared previously. She will have none of it and demands he go back to work. She in turn goes behind some bushes and changes into an old pinafore and immediately joins in the task of piling up the cut vegetation for later burning.

Meanwhile, Joseph busies himself grubbing out the stumps and extensive roots which make excavation difficult. By the time he has cleared a small area at the base of the depression, he can no longer contain his curiosity.

He starts to sink a pit to test for gold. The first three feet consists of clay and loam and although he pans several dishfuls, there is no sign of gold. He is undecided whether to keep digging deeper or start another hole. He describes to Ellen how any gold present would most likely be found in a 'shoestring' lens of sand and gravel, shaped a bit like a very thin, flattened sausage, which could be quite narrow and difficult to find. Once found, however it should be easily traced, possibly for tens of yards along the direction the ancestral stream had flowed. Depending on how rich the sausage is, a small lease like this could contain enough gold to make a man relatively rich. Ellen shows a lively interest in the problem, asking many questions and making suggestions. Between them they reach the conclusion they should dig a shallow trench or 'costean,' perpendicular to the supposed stream-flow direction in the hope of locating a sandy and gravelly section. If it proves unsuccessful, the trench would be progressively deepened. If that too fails, two or three deeper pits would be dug in the most promising locations, as a last resort. Joseph is disappointed he has been unable to confirm the presence of gold but Ellen remains optimistic and her positive attitude buoys his spirit.

    He is amazed at Ellen's physical strength and determination as she pitches in, wielding pick and shovel. Whenever he puts one tool down to take up another, she takes the discarded one and keeps working. She works with him through that afternoon and he insists she stop well before he would normally call it a day, fearing she might suffer too much from her exertions. They wash the worst of the dirt off their hands and faces, then sit together on the stream bank for a half hour to cool down and dry off. She then changes back into her good dress and they make their way back to Stawell. On the way he asks what her parents would make of her helping him in the hard and dirty task of digging for gold. She replies that her parents had raised her to be independent and they love and trust her. Joseph feels encouraged to learn this but is still uncertain as to the way forward. Nevertheless, he feels positive about the future, as long as it includes Ellen.

The next Sunday, Joseph has made good progress with the costean before Ellen arrives, again with a picnic lunch. As usual, she has spent the morning at church, attending an early service and later, teaching a Sunday School class of infants. As her father is the Superintendent of the Sunday School, she can't easily shirk her responsibilities, much as she might like to be at the Pleasant Creek claim earlier. Having discharged this duty, she is free for the afternoon and proposes to spend it helping Joseph. He shows her where the costean he dug has just clipped the top of a sandy patch, amongst the clay, which he feels warrants closer inspection. Ellen insists this should be done at once, even if lunch has to be delayed. Joseph is ravenous but his own curiosity is reinforced by Ellen's obvious excitement, so he begins to dig a pit in the sandy section. He digs in clean sand to a depth of five feet and is beginning to think he might need to line the pit with timber to guard against a cave-in, when his spade scrapes against gravel. Another eight inches sees a change back to clay. Secretly excited but saying little, he shovels some of the gravel into his panning dish and proceeds to wash it in the creek. After the slurry of clay and fine sand is washed away, a residue of white quartz pebbles and granules remain. Joseph scrapes the coarse material over the lip of the dish and with the practised skills he learned first from the Reverend Brenton and then from Matteo, rocks the dish back and forward to isolate the 'tail' of heavy minerals in the groove. Holding the dish tilted towards him, he bends to examine the tail closely, dripping droplets of water from his free hand to separate the heaviest particles at the back. There are two unmistakable particles of gold, much less than one-tenth of an inch in diameter, as well as some finer, powdery grains. He lets out a triumphant yell and holds the pan out for Ellen to see. Her first reaction is a bit disappointing, having expected something more spectacular. She is only partly convinced when he explains the mere presence of gold is critically important and there is a good chance they will find bigger pieces, hopefully even some nuggets, by simply following the gravel wherever it runs within his lease. At the very least, he can expect to recover enough fine gold to build up his bank deposit. Joseph is thinking he will become a man of sufficient means to make him an acceptable partner in marriage in the eyes of Ellen's father but he does not say this. He starts to dream even further, to the time when he will marry Ellen, buy a farm and raise a family. But he is conscious of the reality that much hard work and luck is needed before such an outcome can be achieved and he will need to be patient because of Ellen's tender age.

Joseph continues to work his claim at Pleasant Creek every weekend for the next few weeks, gleaning good but not spectacular gold. He especially enjoys Sundays when Ellen joins him, not only for providing the most delicious lunches he has experienced since coming to Victoria but for the pleasure of her company and sharing the excitement of their success. Each weekend, the claim is yielding gold worth more than Joseph is earning during the week working underground. At this time, reports of new gold finds in the south island of New Zealand are appearing regularly in the Victorian newspapers. Gold was discovered in the north island of New Zealand in 1852 but potential conflict with the Māori landowners had dampened any rush from the rest of the world. Several other gold discoveries were made in the early 1860s but any resulting excitement remained local until Gabriel's Gully was found in the province of Otago on the South Island in 1861. This attracted a frenzied mob of gold-seekers, many from Victoria. Since then, gold-seekers had steadily worked upstream along the Clutha River and its tributaries, locating a new field at The Dunstan and excitement was still growing.

Before Matteo had retreated from weekend prospecting to court Margaret Turner, the brothers pondered whether they should join the rush but lacked resources to support themselves in what could be a prolonged venture. However, Joseph is now building a nest egg which could finance an attempt to join the rush in New Zealand. He was disappointed once, having arrived in Victoria after the main gold rush had subsided but New Zealand presented an opportunity to join a rush not yet at its peak. This could be the opportunity for which he had come to Victoria in the first place. It would also solve his dilemma with Ellen. It would be a valid reason for him to be away for a sustained period, to help him to hold his desire in check and for her to mature enough to be sure of her future. He decides he will quit his job immediately and work full-time on the claim until he has exhausted the sands he is currently digging and treating. This will build his savings further to pay his fare to New Zealand and living expenses for up to twelve months, surely enough time to succeed in finding gold.

Ellen is upset when he broaches his plans with her but she agrees his reasoning is sound. She acknowledges she will need to be older and he will need to brush up his credentials if they are to be married with her parents' blessing, which she certainly desires. Although there is tacit acknowledgement their future will be inter-twined, Joseph is careful to avoid any overt commitment. He realises a long separation involves risks to the intentions of both parties.

Early in November, Ellen turns 14. Joseph is not invited to the family celebration but he takes Ellen out to dinner at the Club Hotel, where he gives her a gold necklace with a heart-shaped locket. It is not the same as an engagement ring, he has not yet met her father but nevertheless it is an indication of his serious intentions.

Towards the end of November 1863, Joseph sets off for Melbourne, embarking on a ship to take him to Dunedin, New Zealand. He has completed the mining and treatment of the alluvial gold from his claim at Pleasant Creek and has more than enough funds to get him to and keep him in New Zealand for at least a year. Reports from the field give him confidence he will find at least some gold. Even if he is unsuccessful, he will at least return to Stawell before his nest egg is exhausted. He transfers ownership of his claim to Matteo. It would be forfeited if no-one is working it on a regular basis and Matteo, who has been envious of Joseph's success, is keen to check if any additional gold can be found.

4

New Zealand - 1863 to 1865

Landing in Port Chalmers, Dunedin, Joseph is immediately struck by the prevailing atmosphere of excitement. The dock area is bustling, with many ships from home ports as far away as San Francisco and Liverpool, loading and unloading passengers and freight. Dunedin has the outward appearance of a staid Scottish city but the pedestrian traffic in the streets is clearly dominated by gold rush types; fit men, mostly young, with sun-darkened faces and hands roughened by toil in the rivers. He thinks he recognises some faces from his travels in Victoria. He even catches a distant glimpse of someone looking like Jake Francis walking with a duo of fashionably dressed women. The aura of a gold rush town, like Stawell, is immediately recognisable but somehow magnified. The people bent on business seem more urgent and those bent on pleasure more carefree and boisterous.

Joseph seeks accommodation for a few nights in a modest lodging and then purchases his needs for the journey to the hinterland, a tent, bedding, cooking and eating utensils, a pick and shovel and gold pan. He also purchases a Miner's Right and finds out the regulations governing the pegging of claims. Each evening he dines in a different hotel with the express purpose of gleaning the latest gossip as to where the gold rush is most intense. There are plenty of diggers found in the various public houses he visits. Many are too intent on spending their recently gained wealth on wine, women and song but he is able to converse with enough of the quieter types to get the information he wants.

This confirms what he learned in Victoria; the focal point of the Otago rush is moving north-west towards the headwaters of the Clutha River. The easy pickings at Gabriel's Gully, the original spark for the rush, to the south of Dunedin, have long gone. The area is now worked by syndicates and companies, using sophisticated equipment to extract harder and deeper gold deposits. He learns that two diggers, Horatio Hartley, an American and Christopher Reilly, an Irishman, who had worked together in California and British Columbia, had last year extracted over 1,000 ounces of gold in just two months, starting a new rush known as The Dunstan in central Otago. Since then, thousands of diggers joined the fray and are still making new discoveries along a stretch of more than sixty miles of the Clutha River and its tributaries. The Dunstan is still producing gold but the newest finds are made ever closer to the Southern Alps, the mountain range running the length of the western side of the South Island. The current focus is a sheep run on the shores of Lake Wakatipu, where a shanty town to become known as Queenstown has sprung up overnight. Joseph thinks, 'surely I will be able to find gold in such a vast area!' After a late supper, Joseph retires for the night, planning to head west early the next day.

Joseph consigns his tent and other equipment to a cartage contractor to be conveyed by bullock wagon to Lower Dunstan, later re-named Alexandra, one of the main towns servicing the large area known as The Dunstan. He himself plans to travel by coach, stopping to visit the iconic Gabriel's Gully which triggered the Otago gold rush. The initial stage of the journey is through lush green, undulating farmlands dotted with fat sheep. He leaves the coach and stops overnight in the small town of Lawrence. Next morning, he walks six miles to Gabriel's Gully.

It is a far different scene to that in August 1861, when it was a tent city of 2,000 men crowded together in area no bigger than a good farm paddock. The tents and men have gone and in their place are a score or so of men mining gold by the sluicing method. One man operates a water cannon, which directs a high pressure jet to break up the hard-packed river terrace situated around the valley margins. The washings are channelled over a sluice box, containing a series of riffles, obstructions set across the direction of flow and coarse 'strake' cloth, designed to trap the dense particles of gold released. The noise is deafening. The water jetting from the nozzle of the water cannon fairly shrieks. Added to this is the thunderous impact of the water as it breaks apart the hard-packed rock, which crumbles and crashes into ditches constantly being re-shaped by men with shovels. Pinnacles of shingle, too hard to be broken away by the water, remain like sentinels as the surrounding dirt is washed away. Three men are busy shovelling to ensure the wash water goes in the desired direction. Two men are loading rocks produced by the washing onto a dray and one man attends to the sluice box. Two others just stand, apparently idle, on either side of the sluice box. He later learns that still more men, unseen, are required to maintain the long wooden water race from a distant stream diversion and reservoir at the top of a nearby hill which supplies the water cannon.

At a signal from a man at the sluice box, the water cannon is suddenly shut off, silencing the shrieking and thundering din. During this pause in the washing, Joseph approaches the sluice box. The two men, about whom Joseph had previously wondered, immediately move towards him, one from either side. He quickly perceives their role is security. Joseph backs away instantly, waving an apology to the guards. When they relax he sees the sluice box attendant pick something off the riffles and put it in a metal box at his feet. As he turns to go back to where he had been standing, Joseph sees one of the maintenance men walking toward him.

'I was just curious. I'm new to New Zealand,' says Joseph.

'We gather a good quantity of coarse gold granules and small nuggets each day. We need good security. Otherwise, it would be easy pickings for gold stealers. We are supposed to be fencing off the whole area soon but the boss says we need more money first.'

'Why did they stop the sluicing just now?' Joseph asks.

'The sluice man probably saw a small nugget. If we don't clean up regularly, a lot of gold will wash away. A lot of families depend on the gold we recover so we do the best we can,' replies the man.

'How are the prospects for finding gold around here?'

'It's been a couple of years since you could make a living as an independent digger around here. Some people are still trying but it is very hard work for very little return. Your best bet is to head further up the Clutha.'

Joseph sees there is no scope for his involvement here but he didn't expect otherwise and is glad to have learned about sluicing for gold in such an iconic location.

After another hour spent watching the process, Joseph walks the six miles back to the town of Lawrence, where he spends the night. The next day he takes the coach again and travels on towards Lower Dunstan. Soon after passing the track to Gabriel's Gully, the coach crosses the Clutha River and runs along its western bank all the way to Lower Dunstan. From the coach he sees groups of tents but surprisingly few men busy around the river bank. The track soon becomes dry and dusty and at times the horses and coach are immersed in a thick cloud of billowing yellow-brown dust. The country is largely bare of vegetation apart from tussocks of yellowish grass and scattered shrubs. Mountain ranges loom on both sides of the river.

Joseph leaves the coach at Lower Dunstan to walk along the Clutha. He is eager to visit the site where Hartley and Reilly had made their find, hoping for an opportunity to stake a claim. For the most part, the river runs through a steep-sided valley with very little alluvium exposed above the water level. Cliffs of bare rock alternate with scree slopes plunging steeply into the swift-flowing water. The only places where alluvial flats occur above water level are at bends in the river's course. These are crowded with diggers. He asks for directions to the place where, just over a year ago, Hartley and Reilly had made their fortune. The men laugh and point to the river. Joseph learns the easy gold exploited by the first arrivals had come from the gravels on the flats within the Clutha River. However, that was in winter when water levels were low. It is now late spring and river levels have risen, fed by melting snow from the surrounding mountains and the alps to the west. The gold-bearing flats within the river are now inundated and too dangerous to work because of the strong current. Many of the diggers who had flocked to the area have dispersed, seeking gold further up the river. Those working here are battling to make a living. The exposed river terraces are hard to dig and yields are low. He is advised to look elsewhere. This is not the news he wants to hear. He is still adjusting to how quickly things change in a gold rush. He returns to Lower Dunstan, despondent.

Joseph's tent and digging equipment arrive in Lower Dunstan the next day. He has them stored until he can decide where he will settle down to work. Taking just a pick, shovel and panning dish he sets out walking northwards along the Clutha, determined to find a location not already picked over by others. On his way north, he avoids the obvious dug-over stretches of alluvium but pans for gold wherever he finds undisturbed shingle on the riverbank. He frequently sees gold but not in sufficient quantity to excite him. He spends the night at lodgings in Upper Dunstan, too miserable to make his usual enquiries about local finds. Travelling further north, he reaches the junction of the Clutha with the Kawarau River the next evening.

Although prospects have not improved, Joseph's mood unaccountably lifts. He still hasn't found where to start digging but the terrain is familiar, mountains in all directions, those to the west still capped by snow. An embryonic town is situated on flat land, on a terrace high above the river junction. He gets a meal and lodging at a newly erected tavern. The staff and customers are friendly. A digger he meets asserts gold is so widespread in Otago it is still possible, with hard work, to recover 10 pounds worth of gold in a week. Although still hoping for better, Joseph decides he will look around within a 40 mile radius and base himself in this area at the most promising location he can find. Over the next few days, he ventures to sites he learned about through talking with locals. He first visits Bendigo, in the foothills of the mountains to the east of the Clutha, where diggers have found gold in quartz veins. The hills are dry, the grass tussocks and stunted kanuka shrubs offer no shade for the hot summer ahead. Dust is stirred up by the northerly winds wherever men are working. This clearly is a place where machinery will be required to prise the gold from solid rock. A number of small stone dwellings already dot the hillside to accommodate the workers settling in for a long campaign. Joseph wonders where they will get firewood for cooking and keeping warm when winter comes.

He next prospects northwards along the Clutha towards the Lindis Pass, where gold was first found by road-workers. This terrain is even more dry; the hills clad in nothing more than grass tussocks. On a baking hot day, under a fierce sun, he finds traces of gold in a creek draining southwards from the Lindis Pass. Working downstream to the east, where the creek emerges from the foothills of the St Bathans Mountain Range, he finds where payable gold is located but hundreds of diggers are already busy in this area. Once again he seems to have arrived too late.

He retraces his steps and ventures to the west along the Kawarau, drawn to the more mountainous terrain. The Kawarau is a turbulent river rushing through a gorge between steep, rocky walls. There is no opportunity to test for alluvial gold, although here and there the river cuts through ancient high level river terraces, composed of a jumble of boulders within hard-packed sand and gravel. Men are working the terraces but it is hard digging and dangerous due to the propensity for boulders, many of which weigh more than a ton, to tumble down the steep slopes. At Gee's Flat, diggers have formed a syndicate to purchase machinery. Towards the western end of the gorge, two fast-flowing rivers join the Kawarau from the north. Narrow tracks climb the steep gradient alongside each river. He learns later these are the Arrow and Shotover Rivers, both with growing reputations for good gold yields. Joseph is tempted to investigate further but continues along the Kawarau.

Emerging from the Kawarau Gorge, the country opens out to an elongate basin occupied by the glacial Lake Wakatipu. The sun shines brightly on snow-capped mountains surrounding the tranquil blue waters. The shores of the lake and the watercourses emptying into it are dotted with clumps of shady silver beech trees. More trees form thickets on the lower slopes of the mountains encircling the lake, interspersed with lush green grass. The air is crystalline, cool and still. Joseph's spirits soar at the beauty of the scene before him. In stark contrast is a shanty town, destined to become Queenstown, at the southern tip of the lake. He is undeterred by the ugliness of the town and immediately decides he will prospect in this vast area. He secures board for the next few days and sends a message to the transport company in Lower Dunstan to send his goods without delay. In the next few days, he roams far and wide with his pick and dish. He finds that gold can be panned almost anywhere from the shingle lining the lake shore but not in any quantity. He traverses the length of the Arrow, Shotover, Cardrona and other rivers as far as the snow line, panning shingle wherever he can find ground not yet claimed. But there are few such areas and the results of his panning are mediocre at best. He laments that, once again, he has come too late.

Eventually, he pegs a claim on the Arrow River abandoned by a digger who left to pursue better prospects further afield. When his tent and equipment arrive from Lower Dunstan, Joseph sets up camp at what is to become known as Arrowtown. He works the river gravels, panning sufficient fine flakes of gold in the first week to purchase a cradle from a prospector who is quitting the field, having exhausted his claim. He settles down to steady, hard work and within three weeks sells sufficient gold to recover his expenses and begin to rebuild his depleted bank account. During breaks in his routine, he looks wistfully at the mountains to the west and ponders when he might have the courage and incentive to explore further from the known gold areas. He is making better than the 10 pounds per week that he had been told was an average return but still his ambition for something better smoulders within.

Joseph lives frugally between his camp and claim all day and usually spends his evenings at one or other of the hotels in town. Even in summer, the nights in Arrowtown are too cool to want to spend any more time in his tent than is necessary for sleep. His favourite hotel, the Diggers Arms, has been erected hurriedly of timber and corrugated iron, much of it second-hand, salvaged from the now deserted Tuapeka gold rush further south. It is lacking in paint and refinement but Joseph finds it a comfortable refuge from the harsh conditions under which he works. On entry, the senses are assailed by warmth and the mingled aromas of tobacco smoke from a dozen or so pipes, stale beer and hot food. There is a babble of conversation, punctuated by frequent guffaws of laughter. Shelves of multicoloured bottles of wine and spirits brighten the unpainted, rough timber with which the bar is lined. A generous log fire provides both colour and warmth. Plum-coloured curtains at the front windows and doors to the kitchen and residential wing add to the cosy ambience. Appetising meals, featuring copious cuts of mutton, are served at wooden tables.

He becomes well known to the other diggers who frequent the Diggers Arms - a polyglot crew from all corners of the earth - England, Ireland, Scotland, America, Germany, France, Scandinavia and even a few Italian-speakers. The conversation centres on gold, who is on good ground, where the new finds are, the all too frequent tragedies such as drownings, suicides etc. After eating, the fraternity of diggers frequently lingers at the bar, downing a few nightcaps before reluctantly leaving the warmth and enduring a cold, lonely night in their tents.

The establishment is run by a rather plump manageress, Mrs Worthington, who treats the diggers as if they were her sons but shows a hard edge if anyone misbehaves. Stylishly dressed prostitutes occasionally visit the bar, adding glamour, tolerated by Mrs Worthington as long as they do not pester the customers. Although Joseph is becoming more comfortable talking about mining with other diggers, he is struck speechless when approached by one of these ladies, who soon realises they should look elsewhere for profit. Such encounters remind Joseph how much he misses the company of Ellen Greene. He wonders what she might be doing and if she misses him.

An Indian summer persists through May and warm, sunny days continue. River levels drop further, aiding the diggers working along the length of the Arrow in the recovery of gold from the submerged shingle beds. Even so, the nights are noticeably colder. Joseph can only tolerate working with the icy stream water for shorter and shorter periods during the day but he continues to recover increased amounts of gold, working shingle beds normally inaccessible. In July, winter starts with a vengeance. Cold cloudbursts dump heavy rain over the lakes area for several days on end. Joseph is mindful of the amount of water stored in rubble dams the diggers have built all along the course of the Arrow River. He senses the danger of flooding and moves his camp away from the river to higher ground. Not long after his move, there is a night of terror.

The many small dams fill to overflowing, unleashing a torrent of water, which breaches the flimsy structures adding mud, boulders, timber and even more water to surge down the valley with destructive power. The deluge crashes into the camps at Arrowtown, carrying with it tents, beds and humans. There is a tragic loss of life. A group of seven young Irishmen are drowned, their smashed bodies recovered up to 50 miles downstream. They include one of Joseph's best friends, Fergus Murphy, a powerfully built but affable man known and liked by all. Fergus had built a reputation as the strongest man on the Arrow, never refusing a request for help when a digger needed some extra muscle to shift a big boulder or log out of the way. He had a knack of striking up conversation with strangers, particularly the more reticent, like Joseph. Joseph is devastated by Fergus's loss, remembering with gratitude his role in drawing him into the comradeship in the Diggers Arms. When the hotel reopens, after cleaning up damage caused by the flood, the atmosphere is subdued, with many former companions missing.

After the rain, snow coats the mountains in the headwaters of the Arrow River and the weather turns frosty. Frostbite becomes the next scourge to afflict the diggers. Joseph spends more time in the Diggers Arms and his nest egg begins to dwindle again. But winter ends early, with a spate of warm, sunny spring days. Then rain returns and triggers avalanches, leading to more devastating floods and loss of life. Joseph dreams of returning to Victoria, where extreme weather events are a rarity.

One evening towards the end of winter, when he has been in Arrowtown for nine months, he is delighted to recognise Ed Clegsworth at the Diggers Arms. It is Ed who had befriended him and had, in fact, rescued him from the underground collapse at Ballarat. Over a few drinks, followed by dinner, Ed tells him that he has been in New Zealand for two years and has managed to put together enough cash to purchase a tavern. He is in Arrowtown to view a potential purchase but has decided against settling here. The big news, according to Ed, is that gold has just been discovered in the rivers draining from the mountains towards the west coast. It is rumoured a party of Māoris have been extracting rich gold from a place called Hokitika for some time. The Canterbury provincial government in Christchurch has been trying to keep it quiet but word was getting out and the proclamation of a goldfield and the start of a new rush was only a matter of time. Most of the members of the government are 'wool lords' and abhor anything to do with a gold rush but opposition to their stance is growing, especially in view of the prosperity that the Otago gold rush has brought to Dunedin. Ed feels his best opportunity might lie in servicing the new rush on the west coast. However, he is somewhat daunted by reports that the sea journey is hazardous and a number of ships have already been lost, together with passengers and crew. A shallow, shifting sandbank and treacherous currents make entry to the mouth of the Hokitika River almost suicidal in the stormy seas regularly lashing the west coast. There is no safe harbour on the west coast and if caught in bad weather, ships have little alternative but to take incredible risks to come ashore. There is no established land route over the Alps and Ed is undecided how to proceed.

Joseph is rapt at what Ed is saying. Here is the opportunity to be in at the beginning of a new rush. It will likely follow the same pattern as the Dunstan; initial activity near the river mouth and then progressing upstream to the source of the alluvial gold, in this case presumably within the Alps. Joseph immediately conceives his potential advantage. As he sees it, the mountains present no obstacle to someone who grew up in the Swiss Alps. He can avoid the dangers of a sea journey by crossing the alps. At the same time, he would get ahead of the rush by being the first to test the headwaters of the gold-bearing rivers to the west of the drainage divide. He explains his plan to Ed and after further discussion, they agree they will go together.

Joseph sells the heavy equipment that would be burdensome on the journey and the Arrowtown claim, which is now known to be one of the most productive in the district. The bare essentials, blankets, basic food provisions, pick, shovel and prospecting dish would be all they could carry with them over the alps. Together with Ed, he then takes a coach back to Dunedin and thence to Christchurch. From there the crossing to Hokitika would be the shortest. In fact, they can travel by coach along the Rakaia River almost to the foot of the alps, so that they set out on foot at a point only 15 miles east of the drainage divide.

The 15 miles to the highest saddle in the mountains take more than five days. Dense vegetation slows progress at the start of the ascent. As they go higher, the vegetation thins but the terrain becomes steep and littered with huge boulders that are difficult to negotiate. Joseph feels at home in this environment and picks his way over and around the obstacles, one at a time. His assuredness encourages Ed, who would never have undertaken a challenge like this alone. Eventually they find themselves plodding through snow, skirting around the edge of a glacier. After several uncomfortable nights spent in freezing conditions, they breast the final rise and see the Tasman Sea glittering below them. A tight cluster of buildings is visible on the coast, presumably Hokitika and there are signs of activity along a wide braided river a few miles inland.

The overwhelming vista is that of a pristine wilderness; a rugged rocky descent to a belt of dense forest on the lower slopes, cut by mighty rivers snaking their way within broad valleys, shaped by glaciers, across a narrow coastal plain terminating in the ocean. The direct descent towards Hokitika looks too precipitous, so Joseph sets out to track along a north-westerly-flowing stream in the hope of a safer and easier passage. He is also keen to prospect for alluvial gold from this point of the journey onwards. Ed is pleased with the more frequent pauses in the journey while Joseph pans the river gravels at regular intervals, particularly at the junctions where tributaries joined the main channel.

On the second day of the descent, Joseph notices that cobbles of white quartz have appeared amongst the darker rocks littering the stream bed. He fills a dish with gravelly sediment and starts swirling and shaking, progressively scraping off the upper layers. Before he completes the process, he sees there is a good quantity of heavy material at the bottom of the pan and his excitement grows. He is surprisingly calm when, on completion, he sees he has panned some coarse flakes and granules of gold. They are still in steep terrain just at the start of the densely forested lower slopes of the range. He has played out this scenario in his imagination many times before and now it has happened; he feels only vindication that his strategy has worked and he knows he needs to think clearly to make the most of his present situation. Joseph starts working back upstream, panning sediments every 100 yards until he no longer sees gold in the dish. Two small tributaries enter the main channel just below this point. Panning of sediments from each tributary indicates the gold is entering the drainage from the western side. Joseph suppresses his growing excitement, although he realises that he and Ed could amass possibly hundreds of ounces of gold by simply panning the alluvium at this location. But what if there are better deposits further downstream?

They decide to conduct a systematic panning of the tributaries downstream for one or two miles on the western side. If nothing better emerges, they could come back and work the present patch, pegging claims if the patch looks good enough. Ed is just as excited as Joseph but they only have one gold pan between them so Ed begins to set up a rudimentary camp while Joseph goes about prospecting. By nightfall, Joseph has worked out that the best gold is coming from the first tributary they found. This stream is deeply incised, with only local patches of sandy material but an abundance of coarse boulders and cobbles, quartz being a prominent rock type. It seems likely that a gold-bearing vein occurs in the catchment upstream from their present position. If so, some of the cobbles and boulders of quartz in the stream would probably contain gold but they have no means of extracting this with the limited tools they have brought with them. The extensive alluvium, around the junction of the tributary and the main stream, offers the best immediate prospect for gold recovery.

For the next two days, the partners work together taking turns with the shovel and gold pan and quickly accumulate about 10 ounces of gold, ranging from dust-sized particles, flakes and some substantial slugs, the biggest of which weighs about 1 ounce. They decide they will need to peg two claims to cover the gold-bearing alluvium near the tributary junction. They will need a cradle to work the patch more efficiently, as well as a means of crushing quartz to extract gold present in the quartz cobbles, which contain visible gold. By this time, they are also running low on food supplies, so they decide to press on to Hokitika to register their claims and purchase what they need.

The journey to Hokitika continues slowly while they negotiate the upper steep sections of the stream. They eventually come to a junction with another stream coming from the mountains to the east and then follow the combined drainage, by now a river, to the west. The valley now is broad and flat-bottomed and the river flows in braided channels through broad expanses of gravel. Joseph pans the sediments here and there and almost always is able find colours of gold. There are immense quantities of gravel but it is not nearly as rich as in their claims further upstream.

Hokitika, when they arrive, is barely a gold rush frontier town, a higgledy-piggledy scattering of buildings made of timber, iron and canvas. A Māori village has existed here for years but activity is in full swing to add the buildings needed for a port and commercial hub to service the main centres of prospecting activity lying some distance inland and north and south along the coast. Joseph and Ed manage to avoid contact with the isolated parties of diggers they have come across en route. However, the prevailing mood makes it difficult for strangers to escape notice, especially those who obviously have been living rough. Ed is determined to sell his share of the gold to the bank, whilst Joseph intends to keep his gold about his person for the time being. At Ed's insistence, their first stop in town is the only bank, inevitably attracting a lot of interest. They know they will be followed back to their find when they next leave town, so waste no time in registering their claims. Only after that do they feel they can relax and seek accommodation in a lodging house, where they treat themselves to a hot bath, a meal and several pints of beer.

Ed looks at the embryonic town of Hokitika with approval as a place where he might like to become a publican. However, he is happy to commit to partnering Joseph in working their claims for the time being, knowing he will be adding to his capital when the time comes to make an investment. They spend the next few days in Hokitika, gathering equipment and supplies needed to work their claims. Eating cooked meals and sleeping in comfortable beds is heavenly after their punishing trip but the partners are nevertheless impatient to get back to work their claims. The biggest question is how to transport their equipment and food supplies over the difficult terrain back to the claims. A tent, cradle, dolly-pot for crushing quartz, bedding, cooking equipment and food supplies are more than they can manage by themselves. The best solution they can come up with is to hire a wagon to take the load as far as the river junction, make a depot and then progressively port it on their backs the rest of the way to the claims.

As expected, they are followed by a small contingent of gold-seekers as they make their way back to the claims. They feel secure they have registered their claims but have lingering doubts they may have not picked up the best prospect along the course of the river. Once they pitch camp and start work, this thought evaporates as they begin to recover the rich pickings. Within a week they accumulate 30 ounces. Six weeks later they have over 300 ounces, more than they initially aimed for. The alluvial gravels are still yielding good gold so they are reluctant to quit the claims. They decide that Ed will return to Hokitika to bank the gold and return with fresh food supplies. The amount of gold they are recovering has convinced Joseph of the need to sell to the bank. They decide the funds from all gold sold will be credited to Ed's account and he will later transfer fifty per cent to Joseph's account. Ed is to bring receipts, documenting all transactions, while Joseph continues working the claim and hopefully thwarting any potential claim-jumpers. Ed finds that the enterprising waggoner who brought their initial load to the river junction now operates a regular supply run to bring fresh food to the junction. There is even a rough track alongside the river. The fossickers that had followed them from Hokitika have peeled off at various points along the track, where they are attempting to replicate the partners' success. Joseph and Ed are not particularly curious about their rivals' success or otherwise, having secured a prospect which has exceeded their highest expectations. However, they are mindful that less successful prospectors could be tempted to stray onto a productive claim and extract some easy gold if the owners are not active.

Six months later, the partners have worked through the best of the alluvial and are tempted to return to civilisation and enjoy the fruits of their success. Joseph intends to carry back a small proportion of his share with him to Victoria. They have crushed many quartz cobbles and found some that contained rich networks of gold. Joseph follows the trail of quartz fragments up the gully to the point where they ceased and prospects the surrounding hills, finding an outcropping quartz vein containing rich seams of gold. They dislodge some quartz from the outcrop and dolly gold but they realise exploitation of this resource would require the use of explosives and heavy machinery. This is not a task they are competent with or keen to undertake, so they peg a claim over the outcrop with the intention of selling it to a syndicate or company.

The final trip to Hokitika is undertaken in high spirits. The partners have succeeded beyond their wildest dreams. The proceeds of gold sales are lodged in Ed's bank account and Joseph watches with some suspicion while a bank official and Ed organise the transfer of his share of the funds to his own account in Victoria. Joseph, with characteristic distrust of large bureaucratic organisations also retains 200 ounces of gold, planning to carry it with him on the journey back to Stawell. He has complete trust in the integrity of Ed, however, who undertakes to manage the sale of their claims and equipment and forward Joseph's share in due course. There follows a lavish dinner to celebrate their success. Ed has determined to invest in business on the west coast and intends to look for opportunities to the north, east and south of Hokitika, where gold-seekers are now active over a wide front. Joseph also fancies the life of a publican or farmer but admits to himself that his priority is to see where he stands with Ellen Greene and her family. The two friends wish each other good fortune and part, determined to stay in touch. Shipping on the west coast is still hazardous but the weather has been benign for several weeks and Joseph secures a passage on a ship bound for Melbourne at short notice. He is impatient to be back in Stawell and determine the shape of the next phase of his life.

5

Stawell - 1865 to 1871

Throughout the voyage across the Tasman Sea and as he travels overland from Hobsons Bay towards Stawell, Joseph's mind is racing. Will Ellen still be unattached and interested in him? If so, will he be able to navigate through the many obstacles to their union? He goes through the list of the potential deal-breakers. Will she still want him? Will her father approve of him? What about their religious differences? What will he need to do to maximise his chances of achieving his objectives?

Joseph decides to be cautious and not rush to Ellen straight away. His first port of call is to catch up with his brother Matteo, who became engaged while Joseph was in New Zealand. They meet at their old haunt, Judd's Hotel. Joseph brings Matteo up to date with his New Zealand venture but Matteo can talk of little else but his forthcoming marriage to Margaret. Joseph mentions his interest in Ellen Greene and the rather radical idea of marrying a Protestant. Matteo says that won't matter as long as it is in the Catholic Church and the children are brought up as Catholics. Joseph thinks this is an unlikely scenario but doesn't pursue the subject further.

Joseph had expected to spend a couple of hours chatting and drinking but Matteo is uncharacteristically abstemious and towards 7pm, makes his excuses and heads off to Margaret's home. In spite of the late hour and his earlier intention not to rush, Joseph wanders into Tippett's Tea Rooms where Ellen had been working before he left for New Zealand. To his immense disappointment, she is nowhere to be seen. He orders a meal and enquires of the waitress, 'Where is Ellen Greene, who used to work here?' The reply stuns him. She had returned with her parents to their farm in Beaufort, some 20 miles to the east of Stawell, which he'd passed through on the way to Stawell. When he thinks about it, he hasn't written to her at all since he had left Queenstown six months ago and it is not surprising that she is not in Stawell expecting his return. Has his lack of communication signified a lack of interest on his part? Joseph worries he might have snatched defeat from the jaws of victory.

Next day, Joseph hires a horse and sets out for Beaufort. It is a small settlement and his enquiry at the town store quickly results in directions to the Greene's farm. It is evening when he knocks on the door and it is opened by a tall serious man, whom he recognises as Ellen's father, Austin. Joseph is flummoxed! He hasn't bargained on a face-to-face meeting with Mr Greene at this stage. He expected to speak to Ellen first, ascertain her position and jointly plan a campaign to win Austin's approval of him as a prospective son-in-law. Haltingly, he introduces himself as a friend of Ellen's and asks if he can talk to her. Austin appears somewhat reluctant to grant Joseph's request but before he can speak, Ellen comes rushing to the doorway from within the cottage. He can see from her expression that he need not have worried about her affection. She is beaming and only just manages to stop herself from throwing herself at him. She says to her father,

'This is Joseph that I have told you about, back from New Zealand.'

Austin replies, 'Well, you had better come in.'

Before they can move into the house, the doorway is crowded as Mrs Greene and four children of assorted ages gather around.

Sarah Greene says, 'So this is Joseph we've all heard so much about.'

Austin says, 'Not me, you'd better enlighten me. Inside everyone, let's get Joseph something to eat.'

The family were obviously eating their evening meal when Joseph arrived. Ellen sets an extra place at the table and Sarah piles some boiled potato and cabbage onto a plate and took a little mutton from each of the half-eaten meals of the other family members. Joseph realises he is hungry and has just crammed a good forkful into his mouth, when a volley of questions is directed at him, 'When did you get back? How was New Zealand? Did you find some gold? Where did you get a name like Mazzucchelli?'

Joseph pauses for a good few seconds while he chews and swallows, then readies himself to answer as best he can. Before he can speak, Austin demands attention.

'It seems that something has been hatching here that I don't know much about. Please tell me all about yourself, where you come from, your family, what you have been doing since you came to Victoria, what you did in New Zealand and what are your future intentions, particularly with respect to our Ellen.'

Joseph recounts his story, starting with his family and how he became interested in geology in the Swiss Alps, how an English clergyman directed his interest to Victoria, his brother Matteo, who he was careful to call 'Matthew' and his experiences in prospecting and mining in Victoria. When he comes to his New Zealand venture, he downplays the extent of his financial success. He suspects he might already be wealthier than the father of his intended but now is not the time to reveal such information. With regard to his future, he says he plans to take a mining job in Stawell and continue as a part-time prospector as time allows.

The tricky bit is what to say about Ellen. He feels sure from her expression and glances she is as committed to him as he is to her, so he abandons caution and says, 'I have loved your daughter since before I went to New Zealand. I have been thinking of and missing her every day and would now like your permission to court her.'

He sees from the corner of his eye that Ellen is beaming. He fully expects Austin to reject his proposal outright but instead Ellen's father pauses for a while in reflection, while Sarah ventures a few thoughts helpful to Joseph's cause. 'Ellen has told me a lot about Joseph and I believe they are very well matched. We haven't said much to you because Joseph was away indefinitely. Ellen was very young when he left and I think they both recognised the need for time before deciding if their relationship was serious. I know from Ellen's side that she has not wavered in the year that Joseph has been away. It seems Joseph feels the same.'

Austin addresses Ellen, 'Are you sure you want to be engaged to Joseph? You are still very young.'

To which Ellen replies, 'I knew Joseph would be my husband before I was 14. I don't mind how long I have to wait. I just hope he never leaves me again.'

Austin seems to gather his thoughts before replying, 'Very well. I consent to an engagement but it will not be a short one. Ellen is still too young to marry and there are a lot of things to consider before we cross that bridge. One thing I can stipulate now, quartz mining underground is too dangerous for the future husband of my daughter. Apart from accidents, which happen far too often, we are beginning to realise the air you breathe underground ruins your lungs. If you must work in mining, I would like you to engage in a pursuit keeping you at the surface. I suggest you consider work as an engine driver. I believe I can help you obtain a job as an apprentice with the company I work for.

Joseph can hardly believe how well his evening, which he thought would be a disaster, is turning out.

But Austin hasn't finished, 'The biggest problem I see is the question of religion. I presume you are a Roman Catholic. Ellen has been raised in the Protestant tradition. We won't discuss this now but you and Ellen will have to settle the question as to where you will marry and how you bring up your children? I can't promise that I will take kindly to a bunch of Catholic grandchildren but that's for you two to decide.'

As if sensing the need to lighten the mood, Ellen leaps out of her chair and hugs first her father and then, more passionately, Joseph. Sarah also arises and embraces Austin and pecks Joseph on the cheek. Austin then offers Joseph his hand and says to the children, who have been following the exchanges in stunned silence' 'It seems our family is set to grow. Welcome your future brother-in-law.'

After further questioning, over a pot of tea, Ellen beckons to Joseph to follow her outside. She links her arm in his and directs him to walk back towards the township. He is still in a state of shock and mutters an apology for bungling what he had intended as a carefully staged campaign to gain first hers and then her parent's consent for their engagement.

'Don't be silly. I couldn't be happier. I told you my parents trust me and respect my judgement. I love my father even more for the way he accepted you and my mother for helping to steer him in the right direction. He may appear stern to you but he is very loving and reasonable.

By this time, they are amongst a stand of eucalyptus trees, invisible from the farmhouse. She wraps her arms around him and kisses him full on the lips.

Joseph asks whether the family is intending to return to Stawell.

'Yes. Father has just come back to the farm to engage a new farm-hand and check up on a few things. We are going back to Stawell next weekend so the children can start the new school term.

After more conversation, alternating with caresses, Ellen asks Joseph to walk her back to the house and kisses him good night. Joseph returns to his lodging in the town, marvelling yet again at his good fortune.

And so, the engagement commences. The Greenes resume their occupations in Stawell; Austin with the Mariners and Sloanes gold mining company; Ellen at Tippett's Tea Rooms and Sarah looking after the younger children at home. True to his word, Austin persuades his manager to employ Joseph as an apprentice engine driver. As the mines chase the gold-bearing quartz veins deeper into the earth, steam engines are rapidly replacing horse-drawn whims supplying the energy needed to lift and crush the broken ore, pump water and transport miners up and down the shafts. The engine drivers are regarded as skilled tradesmen and Joseph is working towards a certificate, which will eventually entitle him to membership of the Amalgamated Certificated Engine Drivers' Association, a highly respected craft guild. At the same time, he is aware Austin has skilfully manoeuvred him into a position where he can monitor his character and aptitude for hard work. Fortunately, as time goes on, both men develop respect and affection for each other.

On the first Saturday after their return to Stawell, Joseph takes Ellen to a jewellery shop and together they choose an engagement ring. Ellen is obviously attracted to a diamond ring but on hearing the price, thinks it will be too expensive and tries to convince Joseph they should buy a more modest design. Joseph insists they purchase the one she has chosen first and assures her they can afford the best. He later confesses the true status of his finances, which will enable them to buy a house when they marry and even invest in a business or farm.

The long courtship goes smoothly enough. Outside of work, Joseph and Ellen spend much of their time together, particularly weekends. Joseph is a frequent visitor to the Greene family home and he often accompanies the family on walks in the parks or excursions to Halls Gap, a holiday destination in the Grampians Mountains. He works diligently during the week, learning the trade of engine driving on the Mariners and Sloane's quartz mining enterprise. His friendship and respect for his future in-laws grows. Ellen manages to change her working hours at Tippett's Tea Rooms so she can spend more weekend time with Joseph.

Over the course of the next months and years, at work and at family occasions, Austin becomes a mentor and father figure to Joseph. One summer Sunday, after lunch, Joseph is sitting with Austin under a shady gum tree in the back yard of the Greene's rented house in Stawell, while Ellen and the rest of the family are cleaning up in the kitchen. Austin starts talking about prospecting and mining.

'I enjoyed my time as a prospector but I've moved on. I am happy I found enough gold to buy the farm at Beaufort. I don't need to be rich, just enough to give my family a comfortable life. If I didn't have work on the mine, we could just about survive at the farm but I enjoy working at the mine and have the farm as security if bad times come. I need all my time outside working hours now to enjoy my family, do my little bit to serve the Lord and manage the farm.'

Austin goes on to share his experiences at the Fiery Creek rush. 'There is no feeling like the excitement you feel when you latch onto a good patch of gold, especially if it comes after a long stint toiling in barren ground.

Joseph replies, 'I agree but the other feeling I enjoy is that of expectation, when I feel I know where to look and am sure I will find a good patch. Of course, I have been wrong many times more than I have been successful. But it doesn't take long after a failure before that optimism returns.'

Austin is already aware from previous conversations and from the ring Ellen wears, that Joseph has experienced success in his New Zealand venture but has no detailed knowledge of his financial status.

'When I mined the rich alluvials in New Zealand, I would often ask myself if I am being greedy?' Joseph continues.

'You worked hard for very little return for a long time before you got onto your rich patch. You developed your skills and you took great risks. You even risked your life, from what you have told me. I think you well and truly earned your success,' offers Austin.

After a pause, Austin asks, 'Have you ever thought about the morality of extracting riches from the earth?'

'Well, man has been doing that from the beginning of time,' replies Joseph.

'True,' says Austin. 'In fact, we traditionally measure the progress of mankind by the materials we dig from the earth to use for our tools. First there was the Stone Age, then the Bronze Age and then the Iron Age. The Romans and Phoenicians mined copper and tin in Cornwall and Spain to make bronze. Where would we be now if we didn't have iron for the machines we use at the mines or the bigger ships that are now plying the oceans? And we mine coal to power both of them. Gold has been valued as a store of value and for adornment, from earliest times. It is called the royal metal because in the past, it was generally reserved for kings and queens and their hangers-on. What has changed is the common man has now been able to find it in new lands such as America, Australia, South Africa, Brazil and New Zealand. It has enabled many men, who would otherwise be condemned to a peasant existence, to become independent.'

Joseph nods in agreement.

'Another way to look at the question is supply and demand,' continues Austin. 'The prospector and miner just satisfy a demand. The demand for gold is created by wealthy people and governments. Gold coins have been used as money for ages and gold sovereigns are still in circulation here. Now that governments issue banknotes they need a store of gold as a tangible backing so people can trust their paper money.'

'You know I am a religious man. I have spent some time poring through the Bible looking for what it says about mining. In the book of Deuteronomy, Chapter 8, the Israelites say in effect, "It's all right to get rich from mining as long as you don't forget the Lord your God"'.

Joseph says, 'I don't disagree with anything you say but I am still fascinated by the thrill of the chase. I want to keep on fossicking but if I find more than I need it would be nice to be able to help people who need it more than me. Do you know my brother Matthew and I have been sending money to Poschiavo to help our family ever since we have been here?'

'I think you will find Ellen will keep you up to that ideal,' said Austin.

Joseph and Ellen enjoy prospecting in the alluvial diggings along Pleasant Creek and Deep Lead but this becomes more an occasional recreational pursuit than an obsession. Both areas have been well picked over for more than a decade and Joseph recognises the chances of a significant gold find have diminished, almost to the point of futility. Nevertheless, his finely honed prospecting skills still enable him to locate a few ounces of the precious metal every now and then and they both enjoy being in the open air and the thrill of the chase. Ellen is not just a companion and meal-provider in their prospecting activities. She becomes a keen observer of the terrain, suggesting likely trap-sites where gold might accumulate. She is happy to take her turn on the shovel and becomes even more skilled in gold panning. In short, she becomes a full partner in the prospecting side of their relationship, acquiring her own Miner's Right, which entitles her to prospect and peg claims. The one activity she does on her own is her weekly attendance at church.

Their desire for each other is abundantly clear. Whenever they find themselves sufficiently secluded, they enjoy embracing with passion. Little by little, they come to know and love every contour of each other's body. But Ellen is resolutely determined to defer the ultimate intimacy until their marriage. Although Joseph is impatient to go further, he is content to follow her lead, confident in the future that awaits him.

Discussions with Ellen frequently return to the matter of religion. Joseph is not religious but persists in the view that the Roman Catholic faith is fundamental and the Church of England, Presbyterian, Methodist and other protestant denominations are misguided breakaways from the true faith. However, his knowledge of the bible and even his own faith is negligible and no match for Ellen's articulate arguments. He has assumed, as has Matteo, that they will be married in the Catholic Church and he knows the priest will insist their children be brought up as Catholic. Ellen will have none of this, although she cleverly argues her case, so that at no stage it causes angst. Joseph's interest has never prompted him to look deeply into the Christian faith but when she argues against a liturgy spoken in Latin, a language neither of them understand, the doctrine of an infallible Pope, worship of Jesus's mother Mary and other matters, she exposes Joseph's ignorance. He realises he had unconsciously resented the priests in Poschiavo when they had told him what he should believe and how he should live his life. He eventually agrees to be married in the Presbyterian Church and bring up their children as protestants. But he cannot be convinced to turn his back on his family's religion and declines to join Ellen's family in weekly attendance at services at the Presbyterian Church. He respects the zeal with which the Greene family embrace their church but he acknowledges himself to be agnostic.

When he reports the outcome of his religious discussions to Matteo, as expected, a storm breaks out. Matteo tries to convince him to change his stance and when Joseph won't budge, enlists the priest to intervene. Joseph is summoned to a meeting, at which he hopes to learn arguments that he can use to counter Ellen's logic. Instead, the priest claims divine authority for insisting the wedding must be in the St Patrick's Church. When Joseph questions this, the priest's attempts to hector and bullying tactics only serve to confirm Joseph's growing disdain for the religious denomination his family had embraced without question for generations.

After the priest angrily terminates the meeting, Joseph feels in need of a stiff drink and goes to the hotel where he and Matteo have agreed to meet. He tells Matteo of his disgust at the priest's attitude and his resolve to go ahead with a Protestant wedding, in defiance of his Catholic upbringing. Matteo is shocked and disappointed at the outcome. Although he inwardly admires his brother's independence, he says, 'You will still be my brother but this will cause a rift between us. For one thing, I don't think the priest will allow me to take part in a wedding in a non-Catholic church.' Joseph replies that Matteo should not allow himself to be dictated to by any priest and that they would just have to get along as best they could.

Three years pass before Joseph and Ellen are married in the Pleasant Creek Presbyterian church. A small group, made up largely of the Greene family and friends attend. Matteo and his wife Margaret, who had married two years earlier, are conspicuously absent from the church but come to the homely reception held in the church hall.

Joseph purchases a modest house in Houston Street, Stawell and they move in immediately after the wedding. Because he earns wages during the week and periodically has a little gold to sell, he still has a substantial bank balance from his New Zealand venture. He has plans for that but he judges that they will come to fruition later.

Their first child, a daughter they name Virginia, is born nine months after the marriage. Virginia dies of cholera just after her first birthday. Their grief is tempered by the fact Ellen is pregnant with their second child, Joseph Alfred, who is born three months later.

Joseph is now employed as a winder driver at the Scotchman's Reef, operating the steam-driven hoist to lift ore and transport miners up and down the increasingly deep shafts, one of the most responsible non-managerial jobs on the mine. His weekend prospecting activities drop off, partly because of the dwindling returns but also because Ellen is increasingly unable to accompany him due to their young family's needs. When they all venture forth by horse and buggy, it is more of a family picnic excursion than serious work. They enjoy just being in the open air, observing nature, without the exertion and dusty requirements of prospecting. On occasions they venture as far as the foot of the Grampians Mountains to the south, camping overnight and marvelling at the lush vegetation and majestic sandstone bluffs.

6

The Hanoverian Reef, 1871 to 1872

Joseph still yearns to make another, bigger gold discovery, not for financial reasons but to further prove his worth as a prospector. This is how he wants to make his mark in the world. His thoughts are turning more to the primary sources for the alluvial gold deposits, which are by now effectively worked out. The source of the Pleasant Creek alluvials is obvious, the quartz reefs on Big Hill behind Stawell, now the bustling, noisy scene of a multiplicity of steam engines, poppet heads and stamp batteries. But the origin of the alluvial gold at Deep Lead remains a mystery. Deep Lead is some 6 miles to the north of Stawell and topographically separated. Joseph and many others dream of finding a system of gold-bearing quartz reefs to the east of Deep Lead, rivalling Big Hill. Such a discovery would establish him as a legend of the gold mining industry and make him a fortune. His prospecting activities increasingly take him to the ironbark forest on the high ground to the east of Deep Lead, looking for outcrops of quartz, which might signify a gold-bearing reef system comparable to that at Big Hill. He is both excited and dismayed when news breaks of the discovery of the Hanoverian Reef on the south-eastern margin of the alluvials at Deep Lead.

Two brothers, Herman and Frederick Kirchner, peg the first lease in November 1871. The discovery of quartz in schist is immediately hailed as the likely source of the Deep Lead alluvial deposits and expectations for a second quartz mining centre in the district are high. When the first crushing of five and a half tons, excavated from a depth of only 12 feet, yields nine and a half ounces of gold, this hope seems to be confirmed.

When he learns about this development, Joseph sets out to check if there is an opportunity to secure any prospective ground in the vicinity. As is always the case with new gold finds, he is not alone. Several parties of men are busy in the area and the nearest unpegged ground to the initial find is some 600 yards to the north. Surface indications of quartz are lacking here but he starts pegging a claim over 200 yards long on the projected line of strike of the reef exposed in the Kirchner's shaft. He has placed stakes in two corners of his intended claim but when he comes to the position for the third, he finds a stake already in the ground. He unwraps the paper bound to the stake and finds his friend Ted Harrison is in the process of pegging the same claim. Each of them unaware of the other's presence because of the thick scrub covering the area. Joseph and Ted worked together on the Mariners and Sloanes quartz mine and both were active on the Pleasant Creek alluvials and they share a cordial relationship. Joseph goes in search of Ted and finds him scratching his head at Joseph's first stake, reading Joseph's claim paper.

Ted turns around to see Joseph approaching, 'So it's you jumping my claim!'

Joseph protests his innocence. When they both realise they each have two stakes in the ground and it is a dead heat, they laugh. The next question is how to resolve the situation. Men are already pegging claims further to the north and it wouldn't be fair for one of them to have to start again, much further away from the Kirchner's find. They finally agree to join forces and form a syndicate to work the claim.

Ted is acting for a group with another three friends and so Joseph is obliged to nominate three others to make up a syndicate of eight individuals. He includes Matteo, Ellen and her younger brother, Thomas. If they were to uncover a bonanza on their claim, there would be plenty to share between even such a large group. In December 1871, Claim No. 5 North Hanoverian Reef is registered in the names of their syndicate.

Prospecting of their Hanoverian claim dominates the weekends for Joseph and Ellen for the next three months. The first Saturday excursion is a grand affair. All the syndicate members and their families converge on the area in a buoyant mood, armed with picks, shovels and picnic hampers laden with sumptuous victuals and drinks suitable to celebrate the inauguration of such an auspicious venture. The sandy soil and rather featureless bush dampen spirits somewhat but they split into separate groups and wander about looking for signs of a quartz reef and finding none, no rock at all. When they gather again for lunch there is an air of perplexity. What on earth could they do with this stretch of sand?

Joseph and Ted are undeterred. They explain they need to dig exploratory trenches down to bedrock right across the claim, which is 125 yards wide and if lucky, they will find quartz and lots of gold. They point out that digging had been required to expose the Hanoverian Reef anyway. They set about enjoying lunch with toasts to the success of the syndicate downed with liberal quantities of beer, wine and rum. After lunch, several of the party settle down on rugs for a nap. Joseph, Ellen and Ted boil a billy of tea and discuss how they will proceed. They pick the site for the first trench at the southern end of the claim and start digging, Ted using a pick to loosen the earth and Joseph shovelling. The soil is initially 20 inches deep and when bedrock is exposed, it is weathered schist, the right host but lacking any sign of quartz. Gradually, other members of the party join in the activity, extending the trench to a length of 12 yards before all heading back to Stawell. No quartz has been seen, either at the surface or in the trench. Ellen pans several dishes of the crumbly schist as well as surface soil but doesn't see gold. Some of the party are clearly crestfallen, but the experienced prospectors, Ted, Joseph and Matteo, realise a lot more work is needed before their claim could be declared a duffer.

The following day, and over the next few weekends, the first trench is extended over the entire 125 yards' width of the claim and a start is made on a second trench. The work is mostly done by Ted, Joseph and Matteo, the other members of the syndicate becoming disillusioned, and turning up less and less often. It is hard physical work and the lack of encouragement even takes its toll on the more seasoned prospectors. Despite this, Joseph and Ellen increase their holding early in 1872 by acquiring portions of the adjoining Claim No. 4, closer to the Kirchner's find, from three individuals of that syndicate who are similarly disappointed with the results of early work.

By the time four trenches have been completed on Claim No. 5 North Hanoverian without finding anything, it is becoming apparent the Kirchner brothers are also experiencing hard times. They have found the northern and southern limits of the Hanoverian Reef, which extend only 10 yards or so from the initial shaft. They have deepened the shaft from 12 to 30 feet but find insufficient gold to justify carting the stone to the battery for crushing. It is beginning to look as if the Hanoverian Reef is not the source of the Deep Lead alluvials or if it is, all the gold has eroded and deposited in the alluvials, which have already been exploited by the early diggers. Ted and Joseph call a meeting of the syndicate to break the news it is time to call it quits. Joseph feels dreadful. He has allowed, even encouraged the novices among the group to dream of fabulous riches, when he and Ted knew all along that the probability of a discovery was low. However, the other members of the syndicate accept the outcome without complaint, perhaps feeling some guilt at how little they have contributed to the venture. They have experienced for the first time the vicissitudes of prospecting, the euphoric expectation of success and the despair and depression when failure occurs, as it does all too often.

Ellen is heavily pregnant at this stage and their disappointment at the failure of the Hanoverian venture is eased with the expectation of a sibling for Joseph Junior. Maria Nastasia duly arrives and Ellen withdraws from prospecting activities to concentrate on the growing family. Joseph continues some desultory work on Claim No. 4, with similar negative results but a new plan is maturing in his mind.

7

The Miners Rest Hotel - 1873 to 1878

The failure of the Hanoverian Reef venture, after so much backbreaking work, has Joseph thinking about pursuits outside of prospecting. The capital from his New Zealand success is still intact in the bank, apart from the little he put into the family house. He has long harboured the ambition to own a hotel, having enjoyed the ambience of the hotels he frequented in his bachelor days in Stawell and New Zealand. He feels there is a need for another hotel in Stawell, particularly where they are living in the expanding housing area to the west of the main business centre. He broaches the idea with Ellen, whose response is lukewarm, to say the least. Coming from a religious family that largely disapproves of alcohol, Ellen has become used to Joseph's fondness for a tipple. She has even come to like the occasional glass of wine, stocks of which Joseph purchases from the Great Western cellars, 6 miles back from Stawell towards Ballarat. However, she objects to the prospect of dealing with drunken louts and the inevitable scandalous behaviour expected in licensed premises. Joseph assures her that he plans to operate a respectable hotel. She will not have to be involved with the bar, he and his hired staff will deal with that. Her role will be to manage the meals and accommodation. Joseph envisages a small, cosy bar, a dining room and accommodation for 10 or so residents, as well as their own family. It takes some time and many discussions to convince Ellen of the merits of this proposal but she eventually acquiesces.

Joseph engages an architect to design and supervise the building of the 'Miners Rest Hotel' on the corner of

Houston and Ligar Streets. It is a modest single-story, timber structure with a corrugated iron roof. The only extravagance is the traditional iron lacework adorning the eves of the veranda, which run the full length of the two street frontages. Joseph's family of four take up residence in 1873 and start their new life as hoteliers. Joseph takes leave from his mining job to set up the business and hire staff, after which he resumes his employment as an engine driver at the Sloanes mine, presiding in the bar of the Miners Rest in the evenings and weekends. He is assisted in this by Dolly, the barmaid, who has been chosen by Joseph for her looks and engaging personality but whose good character is satisfactory to Ellen. A yardman nicknamed Liquorice alternates with Dolly in the bar during daytime which is generally a quiet time in suburban Stawell. The evening bar trade grows slowly but soon Joseph is hosting a convivial gathering of regulars, mostly locals, as he had predicted. Ellen quickly adapts her routine to handle the housekeeping needs of the establishment. Four long-term male guests are quickly ensconced and another four guest rooms are kept available for travellers. The cooking, cleaning, laundry and other tasks entailed with this, added to the needs of her young family, keep Ellen busy, even with the help of a maid.

Both Joseph and Matteo continue to send money to their parents periodically. Correspondence between the families in Switzerland and Stawell is also maintained despite the often six-month turnaround between questions and answers. In early 1873, Joseph writes to his parents, outlining his plans to build and operate the Miners Rest Hotel and speculating that he might travel back to Poschiavo at some time in the future. Joseph's mother replies in May 1873, reminding him he is now married and *'we don't know if your wife would adapt to these towns. You know what the town is like and the woman you have and so you can decide yourself.'* It seems this letter has been written by his sister, Margherita, who is still single and living with her parents. She goes on to say her parents want her to write something else but they are unable to tell her what it is. Her father is sitting at the foot of the staircase, in a distressed state, with her mother sitting beside him, sobbing. Writing on her own behalf, Margherita expresses her disbelief at Joseph's plans for the hotel. She cannot believe he has the funds to do such a thing.

Joseph's youngest sister, Virginia, is now married to Luigi Costa and living in Poschiavo. She has heard of Joseph's intention to come home and in a letter, urges him to come quickly if he wants to see his parents again. *'They are now old. Father is bent and Mother's face has lost its beauty, possibly from crying for her sons.'*

The mood in Prada has clearly lifted in the next letter received from his mother, which begins—

'Beloved Son

Who can ever be able to explain to you our happiness on that day when we received your letter. It was on the 7th November we received the letter and on this day we were just thinking as the feast of Saint Martin was approaching which is the day in which the rents are due and we thought about what we should do, we almost thought of selling the pig to collect the amount which with this we could have paid them and as we did many other times. But suddenly we heard someone calling and we quickly went to see who it was, it was indeed a girl with this your letter we soon gave it to Margherita in her hands and she says this is the hand of Giuseppe and she quickly opened it and finds how much you sent me. Then we exclaimed oh how happy we are with these we can pay for everything and we can fatten the pig a little then we can eat it ourselves. As well as this happiness another one that is that you are all in perfect health this for us is a thing of great happiness. So just think how on that day your rather elderly were truly consoled first however for your perfect health and then also for the 6 pounds sterling.'

This letter continues, explaining that although Joseph had sent them money to buy a cow, the prices at the market were exorbitant, so the money was used to pay off debts. Then a big storm in August cut deep gullies and covered their grassland with rocks. It is now ruined, causing a further loss of income. The letter concludes with what they have learned from Pietro Rinaldi, who had known Matteo and Joseph in Stawell and had recently returned to Poschiavo. He was apologetic because he was inebriated on his last day in Stawell and forgot to say goodbye to their sons. But he assured Antonio and Maria, *'that your wives are so kind and good and so we are very happy. So, we believe that instead of having in Australia only two children we have four and with these six others which with much joy we hope to see them.*'

The next few years pass quickly with both Ellen and Joseph fully stretched to manage their respective roles at the hotel, as well as the family for Ellen and the job at the mine for Joseph. They are busy but happy years, with successive additions to the family, Mabel Lara in 1874, Matthew Ernest in 1876 and Carlo Eduardo in 1878. The birth of Mabel is difficult for Ellen and she takes a long time to recover. This is acknowledged in a letter from Joseph's mother written in July, 1874. She moves on to the subject of debt, *'I can tell you that we do have debts and if you could please be able to send us so much that we will be able to finish paying the lot so that once we have paid them they will no longer come knocking on our door or rather we will no longer need to lower our head when we meet them.'* Margherita writes on the last page of this letter, lamenting her single status and her need to do heavy work in the fields, the mountains and house, caring for her parents. She started ploughing the fields when her father could earn money as a stonemason and now she does it because he is no longer physically able. She concludes by asking, *'what will I do when I remain alone and will have no one who will come to my door and then I breathe a sigh to the Heaven and this is how I spend my days.'*

Happily, Margherita will marry Giovanni Capelli in 1882 and continue to live in the family home so she can care for her ailing parents.

The hotel venture is financially successful and the family prospers. However, the juggling of multiple roles takes its toll on both Ellen and Joseph. Ellen is now mothering five young children and even with additional domestic help, begins to consider the management of the hotel a distraction. She resents that she sees little of Joseph, who leaves early each morning for the mine and spends most of his evenings and weekends in the bar, where he considers himself indispensable as the genial host. Although Joseph tries to limit the amount of alcohol he imbibes, he finds it difficult to fulfil his role as host without participating with his clients, most of whom have become friends. More and more frequently, he comes to bed after closing the bar in varying degrees of inebriation. For the first time, Ellen begins to criticise her spouse for drinking too much and expresses dissatisfaction with their lifestyle. She is on an unstoppable path to vehement disapproval of alcohol, which influences her children towards teetotalism.

Matters aren't helped when Joseph receives a summons to appear in court on a charge of illegal Sunday trading. He had started opening the bar on Sunday afternoons some weeks before, in response to requests from some of his regulars. The Sunday sessions are like a gathering of friends from the local area and are invariably quiet affairs, which Joseph thoroughly enjoys. Nevertheless, Ellen is devastated to be found on the wrong side of the law, let alone the fact that Joseph now spends even less time with the family and has another excuse to drink more alcohol. Joseph pleads guilty to the charge, noting he had thought it was legal to sell alcohol on Sundays provided he kept an orderly house. The policeman who brought the charge confirms the gathering was indeed orderly. The magistrate imposes a nominal fine of five shillings, plus costs of two shillings and six pence for a first offence. Joseph is relieved but Ellen is far from satisfied and expresses the view that they should sell the hotel and move to a home where they can enjoy life as a normal family.

Things come to a head quickly. When Joseph takes up his duties in the bar that evening, he finds none other than Jake Francis among his clientele. It is an awkward meeting for Joseph. Apart from a possible distant sighting in Dunedin, he has not seen Jake since he absconded leaving Joseph at the bottom of the collapsed workings at Ballarat many years before. Jake seems to have forgotten his role in that calamity and greets Joseph like a best friend. It seems he has arrived earlier that day and taken up a vacant room in the hotel. He compliments Joseph on his 'beautiful wife' and family and his obvious prosperity as a successful hotelier. He hasn't any immediate plans but hopes he might join with Joseph in some venture or other. He greatly values his connection with Joseph and has some ideas that might prove to their mutual benefit. When Joseph asks what he has been doing since Ballarat,

Jake is evasive. One of the other regular drinkers at the bar, Jack Bates, says with obvious distaste, 'he's been in the clink, haven't you Jake?' Jake doesn't dispute the claim but mutters something about being framed. Joseph doesn't like the way the conversation is heading and attempts to defuse what could develop into a fracas. He calls for last drinks a little earlier than customary, at which point Jake and several others drain their glasses and head out into the night. After Joseph serves the few customers left in the bar, Jack Bates asks him how he had come to know Jake. He tells them about working with Jake at Ballarat when he first came to Victoria, how he was tricked into doing the dangerous work and how Jake had abandoned him when he was caught in an accident. No-one is surprised by his account and Jack says that Jake is well known for shady dealing and had served time for theft and fraud.

Later that night, Joseph discusses Jake Francis with Ellen. Apparently, Jake had arrived at The Miners' Rest unannounced early that afternoon and made her feel uncomfortable from the outset. He was charming but a little too familiar. He stood a little too close to her for a stranger negotiating the rental of a room but given that he did not mention his previous dealings with Joseph, she had no reason to refuse him. When she learns of Joseph's early experience and what he has learned that night in the bar, she rightly deduces he was the sort of character she had warned Joseph they would encounter as hoteliers. She is adamant Jake has to leave immediately. Furthermore, she has had enough of the hotel business and wants to sell up and focus on their growing family.

That night, Joseph tosses and turns as he considers how he can evict Jake. He dreads confrontation at any time but is sure that Jake, with his charm, will be more than a match for him. Next morning, a Saturday, before the bar is due to open, he seeks out Jack Bates, at his house in

Houston Street. He finds Jack in his garden pruning rose bushes.

'Jack, I was wondering if you can tell me more of what you know about Jake Francis?'

'Why do you ask?'

'Ellen has told me I have to kick him out. I'm not sure how to go about it. I'm dreading having to tell him. Until last night I hadn't told Ellen much about the incident in Ballarat but she thought he was a bad one from the moment he took a room yesterday.

'Well, he's a bad one all right,' says Jack. 'I may not know everything but I do know he was done for stealing gold from one of the mines at Bendigo. He had made the mistake of trying to sneak some rich gold out of the mine for himself. He blamed the shift-boss, who saw him tucking the gold into his coat but rather than speak out immediately, waited until he was back on surface before reporting the theft. He spent time in jail for that. While there, he fell in with some shady characters and stupidly agreed to join them in a scheme to dupe investors. They had promoted a worthless claim near Heathcote as the next Bendigo, enticing a number of gullible local businessmen, who were keen to join the ranks of those adding to their wealth by investing money in gold mining. As soon as they had the cash, the group absconded to another small town, far enough away that another group of gullible locals would be oblivious to what had happened in Heathcote to repeat the scam. Fortunately, the police caught up with them, resulting in another spell in jail. It seems this too was the fault of one of his mates.'

Joseph looks increasingly miserable as he absorbs this information. It is clear he understands the task he must perform but is dreading it.

'What's the matter?' asks Jack.

'Oh, I'm such a hopeless judge of people and I hate confrontation.'

'Francis is not worth worrying about,' says Jack. 'If it worries you so much, why don't you leave it to me. I think I can get him to leave of his own accord.'

'It would be marvellous if you could but I will just have to steel myself to do what must be done,' concludes Joseph.

Later that morning, Jack is among the first customers Joseph serves in the bar. He is full of good cheer and winks at Joseph as if to say, 'It's all fixed.' A little later, a young woman with a baby in a pram enters the lounge bar and orders a shandy at the window that connects through to the main bar. As Joseph delivers her drink, she sees Jake entering the bar behind Joseph's back.

She drops her drink, which splashes over her clothes, as she yells out, 'There's the father of my baby! Stop him! I need to talk to the rotten scoundrel!'

Jake turns around and speedily exits the bar, heading for the accommodation at the rear of the hotel. The woman hurries out the door after him but he is too quick for her. He is heading for his room to pack his belongings but when he sees her in pursuit he keeps going past the back of the hotel, down Ligar Street and out of the town. The woman returns sorrowfully to pick up her baby. Joseph opens the till and presses a ten pound note into her hand.

Jack consoles her as she leaves the Miners' Rest. When he returns, he tells Joseph that he knew Jake had a reputation as a ladies' man and has known of more than one woman he had put in the family way. He learned about the lady who had been in the hotel that morning from his wife, who is a hairdresser. She recently moved from

Castlemaine to Stawell seeking anonymity but would now have to move on again.

    That evening, he relates the happenings in the bar to Ellen. The next day they sort the few belongings left in Jake's room. Any worthwhile clothes are washed and donated to the church, to be passed on to those down on their luck. The remainder are incinerated. Ellen is clearly a better judge of character than he. Joseph puts Jake down to experience and sets about selling the Miners Rest. He already has a plan for the next stage of his life.

8

Swiss Farm - 1878 to 1887

In his youth, minding cattle in Poschiavo, Joseph dreamed of farming on his own land. He realised this would never be possible in Switzerland and had put it out of his mind. Almost all the farmland in the Poschiavo Valley was owned by wealthy businessmen from cities such as Zurich and the farmers Joseph had worked for were merely tenants. They lived well enough, eating the produce from the farm, with few expenses but any profit went to the owners. When Joseph came to Victoria, almost all the arable land was under the control of wealthy squatters, who ran thousands of merino sheep on vast tracts of leasehold Crown land, essentially unfenced, undeveloped bush. Collectively, the squatters were the dominant political power in the colonies and saw themselves almost as equivalent to the English aristocracy, intent on maintaining their positions of influence over colonial affairs.

The principal result of the Eureka uprising at Ballarat in 1855 was the empowerment of the ordinary people, democratisation of the political structure and the weakening of ties with the English colonial authorities. The outcome was not only felt in the gold mining sphere but pressure was also applied to break up the vast pastoral empires and open the land up for small farming. This was done by carving out substantial segments of the sheep runs and inviting selectors to take up surveyed blocks. It was recognised that the productivity of the land could be greatly increased by more intensive agriculture. Land grants were conditional on a defined programme of development, including provision for fencing and clearing. However, the squatters did not give up their land readily. There were instances of abuse of the selection process with 'dummy' selections by agents acting on behalf of the squatters. When such practices were discovered, the grants were revoked. When the land around the Wimmera River, northwest of Stawell, opens for selection, Joseph suddenly awakens to the possibility that he could indeed realise his boyhood dream of being a farmer on his own land.

Joseph made an application to select a block of land excised from Warranooke Station whilst he was still operating the Miners Rest Hotel. Fortuitously, confirmation that his application has been successful arrives while the hotel is on the market. His grant of 320 acres is situated about 6 miles north of the small town of Glenorchy and about 25 miles northwest of Stawell in the Parish of Riachella. Ellen is delighted at the prospect of a farming life, having grown up on the smallholding at Beaufort. They both envisage a tranquil life close to nature, where they can work together, progressively developing the property, as in their early years on the Pleasant Creek alluvial gold prospect. They will produce their own food, keep a variety of animals and enjoy their young family. They waste no time in venturing out over a weekend to inspect their acquisition.

The countryside is very flat but attractive, being grassland dotted with majestic eucalypt trees, much like a park. The blue outline of the mighty Grampians mountain range is prominent to the south. There is no water on the block but a dry creek bed runs past the western boundary. There is clearly much to do. The top priority is fencing, followed closely by a supply of water. Without these, they cannot begin to stock the farm. Joseph starts out to fence his block copying the little fencing that existed on the sheep runs, which was usually comprised of logs and brushwood. Both are available on the block. He supplies the logs by felling trees, at the same time clearing the land for future cropping. It is backbreaking work. The mature trees are retained as shade for the stock but mainly because they require too much work to fell. They decide to accelerate the fencing project by purchasing wire netting, which is becoming available at a reasonable price.

Fortunately, Joseph starts working the block in winter, when the days are cool and more importantly, the Dumnunkle Creek is flowing northwards just beyond the western boundary of the block. Joseph identifies a shallow depression where water is running off his block in the direction of the creek. A well is sunk where the depression crosses his western boundary and provides a good supply of water for stock at a depth of 25 feet. He fences separate paddocks of 120 acres, two of 80 acres and a home paddock of 40 acres. Eventually the farm is well watered by wells in each paddock and two dams. Soon the farm is stocked with sheep, cows, horses, pigs, hens and Ellen is growing vegetables. After a contractor builds a three roomed house and a shed for the dairy, the family moves from Stawell to live on the farm. Rainwater is collected off the building roofs for drinking and domestic use.

From the outset, Joseph's farming venture seems to be dogged by ill fortune. In their first year on Swiss Farm, Carlo dies of diarrhoea or perhaps dysentery, at the age of 10 months. Then, less than four weeks later, Mabel dies, six weeks short of her fifth birthday. She is the third child Joseph and Ellen have buried in Stawell since marrying but Joe, Maria and Matt are thriving and remain a cause for joy to their parents. Soon after the funeral for Mabel, the family is in the kitchen having lunch, when the Catholic priest from Glenorchy arrives uninvited, on horseback. Once seated inside, he addresses himself pointedly to Joseph, dolefully expressing sympathy for the loss of 'your little angels.' He then adopts a more unctuous tone pointing out that the children had been born to a union not sanctioned by 'the church.' He goes on to say the children have not been baptised in the true church. This has dire implications for the repose of their souls. However, for a small fee, he could pronounce a special blessing, which might have the effect of cancelling their sins and ensuring they spend eternity in heaven, rather than the alternative.

Joseph explodes at this. Rising to his feet, he directs the priest to the door, shouting, 'Go to hell with your blessing! My money will be spent on the children that are still living.'

The children are wide-eyed and open-mouthed at this outburst from their usually taciturn father. When Joseph shuts the door and returns to the table, Ellen tells them, 'All is well. Finish your lunch. We have more work to do,' sneaking a wink and a half smile at Joseph.

The priest never comes again. Ellen soon falls pregnant again and gives birth in Glenorchy to twins, Lia and Albert. Lia dies of cholera a year later. The following year Herb is born and three years after that in 1885, May is born. With the arrival of May, they are a family of eight.

In October 1884, a terse letter arrives from Poschiavo, advising the sad news of the death of Joseph's father, Antonio, in July. He was taking a cow out to pasture when he accidentally fell. No-one was within earshot. Margherita was looking after an ailing Maria and helping her sister Virginia with an eight-day old baby. Their husbands were in the mountains cutting hay. When Antonio didn't return people went to look for him. When they brought him back to the house, he was barely alive and couldn't speak. He died an hour later.

A note is appended to the letter, from Giovanni Capelli, who took offence at the remarks of a man attending the funeral. The man had implied that he would advise Matteo and Joseph if he thought the Capellis were usurping the property interests of the Mazzucchelli brothers. Giovanni assured his brothers-in-law that in the past three years he and Margherita had been living with the senior Mazzucchellis, he had only been helping with the many tasks as best he could.

Despite much hard work and many setbacks, Swiss Farm gradually takes shape. While the farm is developing and they can take satisfaction from incremental improvements, life is good. When the development plateaus off after the first four years, they experience some bad seasons. They can see what lies ahead and become disillusioned. In the good seasons, the farm barely makes a profit. In drought years it is a losing proposition. When drought is compounded by animal health issues, the drain on Joseph's capital becomes alarming. Joseph realises that more acreage would be needed to make the farm viable.

Education of the children is another concern. Initially, the oldest boy, Joseph Junior, called Joe to distinguish him from his more formally addressed father, was eight years old and travelled with Maria on horseback to a one-roomed school at Riachella. As more of the children reach school age they become aware of the limitations of the educational opportunities at Riachella compared to Stawell. There is also concern for what the children might do when they leave school. Joe and Maria soon complete the limited tuition that the small school at Riachella offers. Joe then spends his days helping on the farm and Maria helps Ellen around the house and kitchen garden but it is clear as more children reach puberty that more varied options for employment will be needed.

Moreover, the house is becoming too small for their growing family but they are reluctant to spend money expanding the house to meet their needs. Joseph reasons further investment on accommodation was unlikely to be returned if they decide to sell.

Most important of all, they both realise they miss the excitement and romance of mining. They decide to sell the farm and return to live in Stawell.

9

Stawell - 1887 to 1898

While Joseph is engaged in his struggling farming enterprise in western Victoria, the rest of the colony of Victoria continues to boom throughout the 1880s. With wealth derived from both agriculture and gold mining, Melbourne becomes a major city of the British Empire. Fine civic buildings and elegant mansions are built. Gold mining is still generating wealth from many centres, including Stawell but agricultural production is also prospering, aided by a railway network which greatly increases efficiency in getting rural produce to market and ports for export. Numerous banks and building societies are founded to finance the expansion of cities like Melbourne, Ballarat, Geelong and Bendigo. There is an air of supreme optimism in the future prosperity of Victoria. This is all to change in the 1890s.

On moving back to Stawell, Joseph purchases a six-room weatherboard house, situated on an elevated position on Moonlight Hill, at the northern margin of the town, not far from the bustle of the quartz mines. The incessant clatter of the stamp batteries crushing hard-rock ore as part of the gold extraction process is welcome music to the ears of Joseph and Ellen. The land is held under Joseph's Miner's Right; a Miner's Homestead Lease and they feel they are back in the thick of the mining industry. The view to the north is over pleasant wooded hilly country, where the younger children can ramble. Ellen quickly transforms the house to a spacious and comfortable family residence, including a piano and sewing machine.

By the late 1880s, some of the quartz lodes, which have provided the backbone of Stawell's economy for thirty years and rich returns for investors, are becoming depleted. The few remaining mining companies are focused on the deeper, lower grade lodes, with dwindling profits. Agriculture is rivalling mining as the main local industry. The validity of Austin Greene's predictions about the dangers of underground mining is becoming more evident. Many miners are being struck down by diseases of the lungs, due to inhaling dust from fragmented rock, especially quartz.

Joseph secures a job as an engine driver on the Moonlight Extended Quartz Mining Company, within walking distance of the house. The Moonlight Extended mine is adjacent to and owned by the same partnership as the Magdala mine. The combined Magdala-Moonlight Extended Mine is thriving. The Magdala Company was established in 1868 by investors from Ballarat to explore the north-western end of the Big Hill quartz reefs. A shaft was sunk to a depth of 2,140 feet, the deepest in Stawell and intersected several lodes. Unlike the usual flat and vertical quartz veins previously mined, these were mixtures of quartz and fragmented schist up to 50 feet in width and were not understood at the time. None were considered payable. Despite considerable drilling and development, only 28 ounces of gold was produced and the company was wound up in 1883. The lease and plant were purchased in 1884 by two local men, Hobbs and Kinsella, for 700 pounds. They immediately cross-cut into a wide, rich lode and started highly profitable production, which persisted until 1918. The Magdala Company had developed all around the ore body over a period of 15 years but didn't recognise they had a profitable mine. There are many such stories in the mining industry.

Ellen wastes little time before immersing herself in church activities for the Holy Trinity Anglican Parish in Stawell. Joe, now 17, shows little interest in following his father into mining and goes to work as a shop assistant and general factotum in a retail stationery business. Maria, now 15, like her mother before her, becomes a waitress in a tearoom. The younger children, Matt, Albert and Herb attend Stawell State School, later followed by May when she reaches the entrance age. The family settles down with ample time and financial resources to enjoy the best life Stawell has to offer. This includes social occasions and picnics with friends and family and attending sporting events such as the Stawell Gift athletics contest, which attracts the best runners from all the antipodean colonies and occasionally, Great Britain. They take pride in the development of the town, which now boasts fine buildings, churches and pleasant parks and gardens.

One day at the racecourse, walking with Ellen and the children in the park, Joseph encounters a vaguely familiar face. The family are not regulars at race meets but have responded to the urgings of community leaders to support the annual Stawell Cup. Ellen disapproves of the betting and drinking synonymous with racing, but her sense of duty prevails. Crossing their path is a family with two young children. The wife is a well-dressed, elegant woman in her forties. Joseph realises he knows her and nods his head slightly and makes as if to stop and talk. The lady gives a quick look of recognition and immediately looks away and guides the family past, without stopping. Just in time, Joseph remembers it is Iris, the prostitute who had been kind to him in the Ballarat brothel just after his arrival in Victoria. She has obviously become a respectable matron and does not wish to be confronted by clients she has met in her previous occupation.

Some days later Joseph chances on Iris alone in town. He makes himself known to her and learns she had left Ballarat shortly after their earlier encounter and had taken up a more respectable occupation with a milliner in Bendigo. She met her husband there and married. Her husband knows about her former occupation and is unconcerned but it is embarrassing when she is recognised, which happened frequently in Bendigo. They had recently moved to Stawell but she is discouraged by the incident at the racecourse the previous weekend, seeming unable to escape her past. She suggests Joseph might claim he had met her in a restaurant in Ballarat, where she had been employed and thus avoid any future embarrassment, should the families meet again. She enquires about Joseph's adventures over the past two decades or so and thus the friendship is renewed. Joseph introduces her to Ellen in due course and they become part of their circle of friends and acquaintances.

Meanwhile, belief in the invincibility of Victoria collapses in the 1890s. Shares in banks and building societies slump to a fraction of their previous values and many formerly high-flying enterprises are liquidated, paying as little as one penny in the pound of the amounts owing to creditors. High profile politicians, including the Premier, James Munro, are among the directors of the failed businesses, scandalising the populace. These events have little practical impact on the lives of the Mazzucchelli family, thanks to their secure employment. In 1891, Joseph's second son, Matthew, leaves school and enters an apprenticeship with the Melbourne watchmaking firm of Cohen Brothers. After three years he returns to Stawell, where he completes his apprenticeship and is employed as a watchmaker. The two younger sons, Albert and Herbert, both embark on careers in the hairdressing trade when they leave school in 1894 and 1896, respectively.

News arrives from Switzerland of the death of Maria, the mother of Joseph and Matteo, at the age of 82. The brothers, as executors, commission Joseph Rada, a Poschiavo friend, to wind up the estate. The proceeds from sales of sundry blocks of land, the family home and contents amount to 2,864 Swiss francs or about 110 pounds sterling. From this, 200 francs are paid to each of the three sisters. Some of the proceeds are still to be paid in full. The ruined grassland has been offered for sale but no-one appears to want it, the only offer received being ridiculously low. Rada has retained 42 francs for his services and expenses but considers he deserves more. He appeals to the brothers' generosity, 'I know you are honest men and not, as they say, mean.' He hopes to be able to retain more from the final account.

The brothers receive an interim payment of 1,100 francs each. Perhaps the disproportionate amount in relation to their sisters is because their payments from Australia have funded the purchase of the family's assets or perhaps it was normal, at that time, for the male beneficiaries to inherit the major share.

In 1891, Joseph is approached by the mine manager for the Stawell Amalgamated Scotchman's and Cross Reefs Quartz Mining Company with an offer of employment. The job involves greater responsibility and higher pay, so he accepts, parting on good terms with the Moonlight Extended Company. The new company is hoisting ore from a depth of 1,100 feet and Joseph will be winder driver and in charge of a large air compressing plant that supplies air to eight underground rock drills. Joseph is made redundant after seven years, when the grade of ore becomes insufficient to justify the expense of mining and treatment.

Matteo is still involved in mining and is part of a syndicate planning to open a deep alluvial mining venture on the defunct Pleasant Creek diggings. An exploratory hole drilled by the Victorian Government has located a gravel layer containing fragments of gold-bearing quartz. Matteo, who has never lost his zest for alluvial gold, has contributed seed capital to a syndicate formed by a group of other local diggers. The syndicate successfully tenders for a mining lease on the area.

Construction of the John Woods mine, named after a recently deceased but prominent local politician, commences in 1893 with Matteo as one of the directors. A shaft is sunk, intersecting the gravel horizon at a depth of 72 feet. Excavation of this wash zone yields rich pockets of gold in quantities sufficient to justify mining. Further development outlines a buried river channel almost exactly below and parallel to the course of the present day Pleasant Creek. The first shaft is a simple affair with a hand-operated windlass. It is clear from the early production results that mechanisation is justified. The syndicate raises more capital for this and on Matteo's recommendation, Joseph also invests, as it gears up for an increase in production. A second-hand head frame from the worked-out Heather Bell mine is erected over the first shaft. A steam-powered winder is installed and Joseph is engaged as the engine driver. As the mine workings extend eastwards, the Racecourse lease is purchased for 2,000 pounds. A new shaft is sunk in the middle of the racecourse and a poppet head erected. Excellent gold is found opposite the grandstand. The mine remains in production for over five years, during which a steady stream of dividends is paid to the shareholders. One of Matteo's sons, Thomas, is also employed at the mine. Sadly, shortly after the mine closes in 1898, Thomas dies at the age of 32 of 'miner's lung complaint.'

In 1892, news breaks of sensational gold discoveries at Coolgardie, in the desert some 340 miles east of Perth, in Western Australia. While Victoria is in the financial doldrums, the west is booming. Reports suggest great nuggets of gold are found lying at the surface, waiting to be picked up by the first in the field. Thousands of experienced fossickers clamour to board ships bound for Albany or Fremantle on the west coast and make their way to Coolgardie by coach, horseback and on foot, often pushing makeshift barrows loaded with camping gear and digging tools. Reaching Coolgardie and finding the best ground is all under claim, they fan out into the surrounding area. Within months, a multitude of new finds are registered over an area of some 8,000 square miles.

One such find, made in 1893, 24 miles northeast of Coolgardie, initially known as Hannans, is destined to become one of the richest gold deposits in the world. However, challenges abound. Supplies of fresh water are almost non-existent in what, although well wooded is, in reality, a desert. There are no rivers or freshwater lakes and groundwater is salty. The little rain that does fall, runs off into extensive lake basins, where it evaporates, leaving a white crust of salt. The Aboriginals, well adapted by thousands of years living in such a place, rely on rock holes that collect and store water from occasional rain for their minimal requirements. These are quickly exhausted by thirsty hordes of prospectors and their horses and camels, sparking conflict, which the Aboriginals usually lose. The lack of water has inevitable consequences for health and many prospectors succumb to outbreaks of typhoid and cholera. Water supplies are eventually boosted by the establishment of condensers, which produce fresh water by boiling saline groundwater, using timber cut from the surrounding woodlands as fuel. Nevertheless, freshwater commands high prices and is often more expensive than beer.

Back in Stawell, Joseph's family follow developments in Western Australia with growing interest. Joseph and Ellen make no secret of their excitement that a new gold rush is in progress but lament their age and family commitments mean they cannot consider participation. This affects the older children. In 1893, Joe is 23 and feeling it is time he leaves home and starts making his own way in the world. Maria is 21 and eager for change. Matt is 17 and is now an apprentice with a watchmaker in Melbourne. The discussions go on interminably before Joe finally decides to take off for Coolgardie.

Joseph, realising Joe's lack of prospecting expertise, subjects him to a crash course, attempting to inject his accumulated knowledge of the craft to a rather unreceptive pupil. Joe has formed the view it isn't only the diggers that prosper during a gold rush. Providing the services needed by the miners is often a more certain path to wealth and avoids dirty and hard labour. Furthermore, people involved in commerce in the midst of a gold rush often gain intelligence about new finds that can be turned to profit. Joe's reasoning is to some extent influenced by his employer who had prospered from the initial rush at Pleasant Creek and throughout the subsequent growth of the quartz mining phase. Discussing the Coolgardie gold rush with his employer, it emerges that the latter would like to open a stationery business in Coolgardie but does not relish personal involvement due to his age and comfortable life in Stawell. If an enterprising youngster like Joe is keen to establish a business in Western Australia, he would be willing to help with finance and stock on a partnership basis. Joe jumps at the chance. Maria begs to be allowed to accompany him and to work as a shop assistant in the new enterprise. Joe, with the backing of his parents, maintains he should go alone in the first instance.

By the time Joe leaves for Western Australia, the new gold rush is some four years old. He finds Coolgardie to be a much more attractive and civilised place than he had imagined. Instead of sand dunes and bare rocky terrain expected in a desert, the countryside is wooded with fine eucalypt trees. The soil is a rich reddish-brown and although grass is not prolific, plenty of greenery is provided at ground level by an assortment of shrubs, dominated by saltbush and wattle. Coolgardie was declared a municipality two years earlier and is in transition from the initial tent and hessian village to a typical frontier town, with timber and corrugated iron shops, hotels and public buildings lining both sides of the broad main street.

An imposing new three-storey building of local stone houses government offices and other substantial stone and brick buildings for hotels, churches and shops are in various stages of completion. Although ramshackle camps are still scattered over the undulating terrain, more and more houses are occupying surveyed streets, bringing a semblance of order and progress. When he ventures to the east of the town where the initial rush had taken place, it is a different scene altogether. The areas known as Fly Flat and Spud Paddock have been completely denuded and churned up by prospectors seeking to scrape up every last speck of gold. Further to the north there are crowded head frames marking where shafts have been sunk on gold-bearing quartz veins, which are the hard rock sources for the now largely worked-out alluvial gold. Mobile steam engines are scattered around, providing power for hoisting ore and numerous stamp batteries crushing rock and extracting gold.

Joe rents a newly built but vacant shop in Bayley Street, opposite the Denver City Hotel, for his stationery business and sends word by telegraph to the freight agent in Albany to forward the stock which has been provided by his partner in Stawell. As the telegraph has recently been linked through Eucla to the east coast, he also sends brief messages to his partner and family in Stawell to say he has arrived safely, adding, 'Coolgardie is wonderful'. He also makes contact with the proprietors of the three newspapers in the district, negotiating arrangements to sell and distribute their products. When his stock arrives, by camel train, he is ready for business.

Back in Stawell, the family waits impatiently for more news from Joe. When his first long letter arrives, it is effusive in its praise for Coolgardie. Everything is full of promise. The Coolgardie mines, led by Bayley's Reward, are producing rich gold and new finds are reported every week from the surrounding district, up to 60 miles in all directions. One locality in particular, Hannans, promises to out-shine Coolgardie. The initial discovery, made by Paddy Hannan and his mates in 1893, was a typical narrow quartz vein affair but some two miles to the south, in an area dubbed scornfully 'Brookman's Sheep Paddock', prodigious yields are reported below ironstone outcrops. Joe had travelled by Cobb and Co. coach from Southern Cross but the railway currently being extended to Coolgardie is expected to be completed by the end of 1896. Water is no longer in short supply, thanks to the erection of condensers but it is very expensive. The town is growing in size and the quality of housing, public buildings, business premises, parks and amenities are ever improving. Business opportunities abound. The town is even planning to hold an International and Mining Exhibition in 1898.

Joe's reports even include glowing descriptions of the surrounding bush, although he has never before shown much interest in nature. Perhaps it is the contrast between the reality and what he had imagined he would find that moves him to comment on how agreeable he finds the bush surrounding the town. The eucalypt trees have slender trunks with smooth white or salmon-coloured bark and a crown of glossy green leaves. It is spring and wildflowers of every colour are abundant. He is particularly impressed with the unique aroma of the native hop bush, a shrub festooned with reddish-brown waxy flowers. The climate is mild, with sunny days and chilly nights. Later letters, as summer advances, mention, somewhat grouchily, hot northerly winds and dust storms, often followed by spectacular thunderstorms. Insects, particularly the flies, are also bothersome but not sufficient to dampen his enthusiasm for the new frontier.

In January 1898, Joseph and Ellen are knocked adrift of their moorings by two untimely deaths. First, Joseph's brother Matteo dies unexpectedly. He is still a director of the John Woods mine and seemingly in robust health at the age of 61. Eleven days later, Ellen's father, Austin dies. Both men are very dear to Joseph and Ellen and their loss is a bitter blow. In Matteo, Joseph has lost the only member of his birth family in this part of the world and he has come to regard Austin Greene, not just as a father-in-law but also in many ways, his real father. Joe's letters have strengthened the determination of his siblings to follow him to the West. Matt, Maria and Bert set out during 1898, leaving Joseph, Ellen, Herb and May in Stawell, feeling somewhat abandoned, not to mention envious.

It is not long before Joseph and Ellen resolve to move to Coolgardie. Joe's more recent letters home have increasingly contained glowing references to a certain Selena Rutherford. His latest letter now announces he has proposed marriage to Selena. He expresses the hope that his parents and siblings will be able to be present at the wedding in 1900. He goes further, urging his parents to move the family to Coolgardie permanently. He contrasts the prosperity of the Eastern Goldfields of Western Australia with decline in Victoria. He also advises the International Exhibition in Coolgardie has now been postponed until March 1899 and is expected to remain open for six months. The idea that Coolgardie is planning to stage an international exhibition accelerates their decision. If Coolgardie can mount an international exhibition like London and most recently, Melbourne in 1880, it must indeed be a place of the future. Their youngest child, May, has turned 13 and is ready to leave school and get a job. Besides, the fact that half the family is already settled in the west and unlikely to move back, the recent deaths of Austin and Matteo, are all factors in favour of a permanent move.

On advice from Joe, they advertise to sell up their Stawell home, complete with furniture and travel with only clothing and their most precious keepsakes. They journey by train to Adelaide, where they embark on the steamer *Ortona* bound for the port of Albany on the southern coast of Western Australia. Before the ship sails they have a day to explore Adelaide, admiring the layout of the city, with its rectangular pattern of wide streets, surrounded on all sides by parklands. When the ship sails on towards their destination port of Albany, they are soon amongst the giant swells of the Southern Ocean. Fortunately, the weather is benign and they can spend much time on deck, fascinated by the half a dozen or so magnificent albatross which always seem to follow the ship, occasionally swooping into the wake to pick up titbits thrown overboard. Occasionally they observe flying fish or dolphins, which seem to race the steamer. Five days later they sail into the calm waters of King George Sound and thence into Princess Royal Harbour, on which Albany, the oldest European settlement in the colony of Western Australia, is situated. The little township of Albany seems out of proportion to the majestic expanse of the harbour, with its surrounding granite headlands and hills. From there they travel 600 miles by rail to Coolgardie, via Beverley, Northam and Southern Cross.

The journey by rail is long and tedious, with many stops to take on coal and water but the family is fascinated by the changing scenery. Initially, the journey takes them through undulating green farmlands, interspersed with thickets of bush, which include some of the tallest eucalyptus trees they have seen. As they proceed further north from Albany, the terrain becomes flatter, although there are occasional glimpses of hills and even mountains in the distance. The latter, they are told, are the Stirling Ranges, the highest 'mountains' in southern Western Australia, which is dominated by a seemingly endless plateau. At the same time, the country becomes drier, not unlike the Wimmera, where the Swiss Farm had been located. There are extensive swathes of natural bushland, the development of cleared agricultural land lagging behind that in western Victoria. Occasionally they pass rounded hillocks of bare granite and more rugged hills composed of a tumble of rounded granite boulders. There are stretches of flat, sandy country with a thick cover of scrubby vegetation, the soil obviously too poor for farming and flat-topped hills capped with ironstone.

Herb is particularly struck by the rounded hills seen between Brookton and York and makes a mental note that he would like to be a farmer in such an area. Their northern journey ends at Northam, a small town surrounded by undulating farmlands. Here they transfer to the train heading eastwards to the Eastern Goldfields. The country to the east of Northam is initially similar to that which they have already travelled. The proportion of cleared farmland compared to bush diminishes the further they travel and the terrain becomes even flatter. The native vegetation is attractive. The term 'woodland' seems apt, to describe the liberal scattering of fine eucalypt trees and shrubby understory. Every now and then, they pass groups of men working on the new water scheme from the west coast to the Goldfields. Most parties are laying a large diameter pipeline but several more substantial construction sites, they learn, will become the steam-driven pumping stations required.

The town of Southern Cross marks the start of the Goldfields and they relish the sight of the head frames they can see as they walk around the town while the train refuels. Between Southern Cross and Coolgardie is a stretch of 100 miles without any towns but only a few sidings where the train takes on water. These are usually close to dome-like outcrops of granite, often extending over many acres. They are ideal natural collectors of run-off from sporadic rainfall events. Water capture is enhanced by low brick or stone walls and directed into storages such as dams or wells. From there it is pumped into overhead tanks. The family can easily walk to the highest point of one of these outcrops during one stop. Although it is less than 50 feet above the surroundings, they are amazed at how far they can see in all directions from the top and how empty the landscape is.

The country to the east of Southern Cross alternates between open eucalypt woodland and an extensive sand plain with dense scrubby vegetation and occasional low, stony ridges of ironstone. The soil everywhere is an attractive reddish-brown colour. Anticipation grows as they approach Coolgardie. It has been a long and tiring journey and the family looks forward with excitement to their reunion with Joe, Matt, Maria and Bert and to the next phase of their adventure.

10

Coolgardie - 1899 to 1900

Joe has assembled his Goldfields-based siblings as a welcoming committee and it is a joyful celebration as the train pulls into the station at Coolgardie on a warm Saturday and the whole family reunites. Also on the platform is Joe's fiancée, Selena Rutherford. By coincidence, Selena was born in Beaufort, Victoria and the Rutherford family is known to Ellen. The station building, a substantial edifice constructed of local stone, is a spanking new and imposing introduction to the town, completed when the railway linking Coolgardie and Kalgoorlie to Southern Cross and hence Perth, only a couple of years previously. After the initial meeting, the party adjourns to the town centre for refreshment and a chat. Leaving the station, it is only a short walk, during which they glimpse a town in transition from a frontier place of shanties and shacks to a newly proclaimed municipality, looking to an optimistic future.

They are soon taking tea in the splendid Denver City Hotel. This was rebuilt less than a year ago, after the original had been burned to the ground in a disastrous fire, along with half a dozen adjoining shops. Joe, whose stationery business is on the opposite side of Bayley Street, beams with pride when recognised and greeted by the staff and several of the patrons present. Joe is quick to report his newsagency and stationery shop is doing well and he is chummy with the leading businessmen in the town. Maria is working in a drapery and Bert in a barber shop. All three are living in respectable boarding houses. Matt is employed by a jeweller and watchmaker in Boulder and is dreaming of a partnership. Boulder is a prosperous town some two and a half miles south of Hannans, now known as Kalgoorlie. Boulder is closer than Kalgoorlie to the major mines in the area, which are incredibly rich and promise a long future. Frequent trains run between Coolgardie and Kalgoorlie/Boulder, so Matt intends to stay in Coolgardie until Sunday afternoon. Joe is eager to show the new arrivals around the town before dark. When they finish their tea and everyone has recounted their news, they leave their travelling luggage at the hotel, where they will be spending the night. The bulk of their belongings have been shipped in several packing crates which will be delivered later.

Of course, the first stop in Bayley Street is across the road to Joe's stationery and newsagency, called 'The Arcade.' Joe tells the group his sponsor in Stawell is planning to retire and Joe is hoping to eventually become the sole proprietor of the business. The racks of magazines, shelves of books, reams and rolls of paper, stacks of exercise books, boxes of nibs, bottles of ink and jars of pencils draw murmurs of approval which Joe laps up like a contented cat.

When they return to Bayley Street, Herb can't help expressing his surprise at the wide expanse of the road. 'That's so the camel teams can turn around,' says Joe. He explains that camel teams, together with Afghan handlers, were brought in from Asia because of their ability to travel long distances with minimal water. Camel teams were used to haul most of the heavy freight needed for the mines, building materials for the town and general freight, in the four years before the railway reached Coolgardie in 1896. Now they are rarely sighted and many of the camels were released into the bush, where they have gone feral. Bayley Street is lined on both sides by shops and hotels. Almost all have verandas to shade shoppers from the fierce summer sun and shelter from the more occasional rain. Most are single-storey and of wooden or corrugated iron construction but many of the newer hotels and public buildings are double-storey and made of brick or stone. The family progresses along the street, pausing at intervals while Maria and Albert point out where they work or to admire or criticise, various window displays.

'There seem to be a lot of hotels,' says Ellen, with a hint of disapproval.

'Twenty six, to be precise,' says Joe, proudly. 'And three breweries, as well. There are two stock exchanges and three daily newspapers.'

At the eastern end of their wandering along Bayley Street, Joe points out the imposing three-storey government offices and court house, recently completed in local stone. Ellen wants to know where the Church of England is situated, so the party heads two blocks to the north to Lindsay Street, where they find the modest timber and iron church of St Andrews. Ellen notes the times of services so she and the children can attend the next day. From there they are drawn further west along Lindsay Street by the odd-looking two-storey Masonic Lodge completely clad by corrugated iron.

Joe says, 'A lot of my friends are Freemasons and have invited me to join a lodge. They say it's a benevolent institution based on Old Testament scripture. I am curious but they won't tell me exactly what they do.'

Matt chips in, 'I've had similar approaches. It seems you must join up before you get to know what you are signing up for. A lot of men I admire are Freemasons so I'm thinking I will take it up. I know the combined lodges in Boulder hold an annual carnival to raise funds for charity.'

By this time, the sun is getting low, so Joe directs them further up Hunt Street, past the impressive stone school building, to an elevated point where they can look to the east over The Bluff.

'Sunset is the best time to see this,' says Joe. The Bluff is a rounded hill, surmounted by a steep-sided, flat-topped ironstone cap. It is an intriguing natural landmark, set glowing by the rays of the setting sun. It is a beautiful sunset, wispy clouds to the west turn crimson as the sun goes down. Herb and May want to climb The Bluff but Ellen restrains them. It is time to call it a day and continue their tour of Coolgardie the next day.

The new arrivals return to the hotel, eager for a bath and a change of clothes. When they meet later for dinner, Joseph grumbles about the stingy amount of water allocated for a bath and the exorbitant charge. Joe explains the high cost of water will soon be a thing of the past. The pipeline bringing water from the Darling Range is under construction, as they observed from the train. When completed in a year or so, there will be water enough for parks and gardens. May complains about the reddish-brown colour of the water after her bath.

'You'll soon get used to that. The red dirt gets into everything, especially in summer, when you get dust storms. Then you get a thunderstorm and the streets all turn to mud,' Joe offers cheerfully. It seems no inconvenience will dampen his enthusiasm for the Eastern Goldfields of Western Australia.

Ellen arises full of enthusiasm when Sunday dawns so she can go to church with the family, leaving Joseph behind, who likes to sleep in on Sunday. Ellen is pleased to see Joe with his fiancée, Selena and Maria and Albert, her other two Goldfields-based children, obviously regular worshippers, in the congregation. The little church is packed with men, women and children, who respond to the liturgy with a will and lustily sing the hymns. An intellectual and challenging sermon is preached by Archdeacon J. Barton Parkes. Walking back to the hotel, Joe explains to Ellen that Parkes is the second rector of St Andrews, replacing the saintly Edward Mallon Collick, who recently transferred as rector to St Matthews, Boulder, Matt's parish. Joe is keen that Ellen appreciates Collick's legendary exploits in the Goldfields.

'He arrived in Coolgardie in 1893, less than a year after the discovery of gold, when most of the population were men roughing it. Most of them lived in tents. He conducted his first services in any premises he could borrow, like a store or billiard saloon. The congregation would sit on planks supported by whisky cases. He was surprised to find very few men attended his first services. On further investigation, he found he was competing on Sunday mornings with a popular rival attraction, organised boxing matches. He forthwith issued a challenge to fight the town champion, on the understanding that should he win, the boxing fraternity would be obliged to attend his next service. The local was no match for Collick, who had learned to box in his former parish in the east end of London. It seemed his sermons were as compelling as his fists, for his congregation was soon thriving, particularly as more women settled in the town.

By now they are walking past the three-storey government building in Bayley Street but Joe hasn't finished his account of Collick's exploits. 'As soon as he arrived in Coolgardie, Collick devoted himself whole-heartedly to the community, Christian and pagan, black and white alike. When cholera and typhoid epidemics overwhelmed the nursing staff in the early days of water shortage, he volunteered to help in the hospital. 'Mitter' Collick was also idolised by the Coolgardie Aboriginals for his loving concern for their welfare. Every Christmas he put on a special celebration for them. To start with, they were given the opportunity to wash and put on a clean set of clothes. After a hearty lunch, they took part in an afternoon of sporting events.'

'He must have had a very strong constitution to do all that without getting sick himself,' observes Ellen. 'He sounds like a saint but one not afraid of confrontation.'

'Yes. Most people on the Goldfields are focused on acquiring wealth but Collick gives away everything he has. Before Kalgoorlie had its own church he conducted church services there with the Kalgoorlie parishioners contributing money for him to travel the 25 miles by coach. Once, two of the contributors found him half-way to Coolgardie, walking. When they asked him why, he said he had given his fare to a poor woman with a sick child 'who needed it more than me.' He even gave away the money his parishioners had collected to send him on holiday, to the needy.

Ellen thanks Joe for his account and resolves to attend one of the legendary Collick's services in Boulder when she is able to visit Matt. In the meantime, she makes herself known to the local Anglicans and gets her new 'ministry' under way.

After church, the family changes clothes and gathers again to continue their tour of Coolgardie and the surroundings. They first walk to the mining area immediately east of the town. Joe points out Fly Flat where prospectors Bayley and Ford had picked up over 500 ounces in gold nuggets in a few days in 1892, sparking the biggest gold rush since the 1850s in Victoria. This ground has since been worked over multiple times and every minute speck of gold gleaned.

'I can see from the hummocks that this ground has been well and truly worked,' observes Joseph, 'but how did they recover the gold without a good supply of water?'

'I understand the prospectors here developed an extraction process that they call 'dry-blowing.' I don't know much about it but it is still used in several areas close to town. I'll see if I can find out where you can see it in action,' replies Joe.

They wander to the north amongst the head-frames and stamp batteries of the syndicates and companies mining the fabulously rich quartz veins. Even on Sunday, all is noise, bustle, smoke, steam and red dust.

From there, Joe leads them a short distance south to the pavilion constructed for the International Exhibition. There have been delays in shipping mining equipment from overseas and the inauguration of the exhibition is postponed until March this year. Joseph remarks, 'It's a good thing there is a delay. Otherwise, we would have missed it.'

'The organisers are a bit worried at this stage. They've had to delay the start several times already. South Australia is the only other state to set up an exhibit. The committee is calling on the community to get behind it,' says Joe.

'I'm sure we can help,' says Ellen. 'As long as we know what's needed.'

The building itself is complete. The main building is of locally quarried stone, with an impressive entrance capped off with classical columns and a tower. This houses the administration and includes a concert hall and exhibition galleries. Additional buildings of corrugated iron form a quadrangle behind the stone buildings at the front. This is where the mining machinery is exhibited. It is planned to use the complex as a School of Mines after the exhibition concludes. A full program of sporting and cultural events is planned to be held throughout the duration of the exhibition.

They next walk further south to 'The Gorge' where a creek has been dammed to create a small lake. Many people are already here, dotted around in small groups, having picnics. The boys gratefully unload the food and drink they have been carrying all morning and the family sits down to a late lunch. From there it is an uphill hike to the 'gnamma hole,' a water hole, which supplied water to the local Aboriginals for millennia. This was called 'Coola Carbi' by the indigenous people. They had been willing to share this precious resource with the first twenty or so diggers but when hundreds and then thousands of Europeans and their horses wanted to use it, their consternation was understandable. Later, explosives were used in a misguided attempt to get the gnamma hole to yield more water. It was here in 1894 that Warden Finnerty had proclaimed the Municipality of Coolgardie, getting the name the Aboriginals used slightly wrong.

Finally, the family walks further up the gentle slope, passing the impressive house of Warden Finnerty to a hill commanding expansive views of the whole town, mining area and the bush beyond. Here, Joe speaks with due reverence about Finnerty. He has presided as the ultimate authority figure in Southern Cross and then Coolgardie from the very early days of the field. He fulfils the dual roles of mining warden, exercising judgement on matters under the Mining Act and magistrate for civil and criminal justice. He is, in effect, the senior representative of the Colony of Western Australia on the Eastern Goldfields and has exerted a positive influence throughout the most exciting and turbulent years of their development. He was instrumental in the provision of supplies of water along the track to and in Coolgardie during the early stages of the gold rush. He had ordered all diggers to return to Southern Cross during the first summer of the Coolgardie rush in 1892, when the dearth of stored water would otherwise have led to many deaths. His administration of the Mining Act contributed greatly to the development of mines by facilitating the investment of English capital.

At the end of the day, the family is tired but well satisfied with what they have seen and keen to activate the next stage of their lives.

Within two weeks, Joseph and Ellen purchase a typical home in Lindsay Street. It is a step down from the home they left in Stawell but the housing market is still tight in Coolgardie and nothing better is available at this time. Joseph promises Ellen they will upgrade as soon as possible. Ellen is not unhappy with the purchase, mainly because it is in the same street close to the Anglican Church. It is a timber and corrugated iron construction, with the inside rooms lined with hessian smeared with quicklime and painted to brighten the interior. Being mid-summer, it is not long before the family discovers the house is stiflingly hot in heatwaves, when maximum temperatures exceed 100 degrees Fahrenheit in the shade for several days on end. They soon realise the best place for relief when the heat in the house becomes unbearable is outdoors. There are several mature salmon gum trees in the yard which provide dappled shade. The previous owners of the house planted two peppercorn trees in the back yard. These are, as yet, small but promise to provide an extensive shaded area as they mature. Precious water from the bath, sink and laundry troughs is devoted to their rapid growth. On the hottest nights they often sit outdoors, enjoying the velvety warmth and marvelling at the brilliant spectacle of the constellations of stars sparkling in the clear, still air. Another godsend in hot weather is the 'Coolgardie safe,'

an ingenious cupboard-like construction with an outer covering of hessian which is dampened and with the help of any breeze, keeps food cool in the extreme summer temperatures. Invented locally by Arthur McCormick, all homes in the Goldfields have one of these, usually on the back veranda, close to the kitchen. Also, on the veranda hangs a canvas water bag, a source of cool drinking water for the whole family.

The house has four main rooms, two on each side of the passage which traverses the house from the front porch to the back veranda. On one side of the passage are the parlour and kitchen, with interconnecting doors. On the opposite side of the hall are two bedrooms, the parents' bedroom at the front, with casement windows looking out onto Lindsay Street, the girls at the back with a window to the east side. Maria moves back to live with the family and shares the bedroom with May. Albert and Herb sleep on the back veranda. As at Swiss Farm, the kitchen is the focal point for family life. A large kettle is kept simmering on the Metters wood stove to provide water for washing, bath water and frequent pots of tea. Ellen coaxes delicious meals from the stove, which are consumed at a large table. On one side of the back veranda an enclosed area contains an iron bathtub and wash-basin. On the other side is a copper tub set over a brick fireplace and troughs for washing clothes. The lavatory is a separate structure backing onto a lane at the rear of the block. When they arrive, this is a primitive timber outhouse built over a hole in the ground. A scoop of ash is dropped down the hole after each use. Periodically, kerosene is tipped over the waste and ignited. This system is later superseded by the night cart. A trapdoor opens onto the lane, through which the sanitary man removes the can of waste once a week, replacing it with an empty can.

Despite the spartan construction, Ellen and Joseph make the house attractive and comfortable by means of simple home furnishings. Ellen is adept at making the most basic shelter into a comfortable home and works diligently at this task, finding that the shops in Coolgardie have good stocks of the necessities for home furnishings and family life, including a piano, replacing the one they had sold in Stawell.

Joseph finds employment as an engine driver at the Bayley's United Mine, the deepest shaft on the field. He had joined the Amalgamated Certificated Engine Drivers' Association in Stawell, when it was first formed in 1897 and his membership of this prestigious craft union, together with references from his previous employers are helpful in gaining a position as a winder driver. Street processions to mark special occasions usually include the various craft unions marching behind colourful banners. Joseph is proud to join in behind the banner of ACEDA. Maria helps May to find a job as a waitress. Herb is employed as a barber at the same shop where Albert works. Joseph and Ellen soon find themselves presiding over a small household, with only Albert, Herb and their two daughters, Maria and May living at the Lindsay Street home. Joe is making plans to marry next year and lives at the rear of his shop.

Once they acclimatise, they find summer not overly oppressive and enjoy evening walks around the town and suburbs. They take particular interest in what people have done to beautify their homes and gardens given the shortage of water and harsh climate. On weekends they venture further afield, into the surrounding bush, often taking a picnic lunch. They are struck by the varieties of eucalypt trees which are clearly adapted to the arid conditions. The biggest and most majestic trees are the salmon gums. These have shiny, smooth salmon-coloured bark and glossy green leaves. Then there is the lemon flowering gum, which has bluish-green leaves and a weeping habit and the coral gum, with dark rough bark and small pink flowers. One of the most striking is the gimlet tree, which has ramrod straight trunks and limbs, with a ropy, fluted structure.

Joseph recalls seeing constructions in the yards of numerous houses in Coolgardie built with the trunks and limbs of gimlet trees. He conceives the idea of building a shade-house with materials from the bush surrounding Coolgardie, copying from examples he has seen, walking around town. With the help of his sons, the shade-house is soon completed, using gimlet logs for the frame. Across the top, supporting the brushwood thatch, Joseph uses saplings of other eucalypts, which grow in dense thickets of slender, straight poles. The top half of the western wall is thatched to provide shade from the late afternoon sun but the other three sides are left open to allow the passage of any cooling breeze. All tied together with wire to resist damage from 'willy-willies', miniature tornados that criss-cross the area, raising twisting columns of dust and debris. Joseph has ensured the shade-house is well away from the house, which radiates heat on sunny summer days. It is a great success and the family regularly spend time in it, talking or reading on hot days and nights. Ellen sees the possibility of other useful structures made of bush timber, such as a trellis bordering the back veranda over which to grow a shady creeper or, when the water comes, a grape vine.

One Saturday afternoon, Joseph, Ellen, Herb and May take the train to Kalgoorlie to visit Matt and find out how he is faring. They have arranged to spend the night at the Albion Hotel in Boulder, conveniently close to Matt's employment in Lane Street, primarily so Ellen can attend a service conducted by the legendary Reverend Collick. Matt meets them at the train station in Kalgoorlie and they take a horse-drawn coach to Boulder. Matt explains that soon there will be two alternative forms of transport between the twin towns, a loop-line railway, connecting some dozen localities around Kalgoorlie and Boulder and an electric tram service. After showing them Manhire's Jewellery and Watchmakers business, where he works, Matt takes them on a tour of the Burt Street shopping precinct. At dinner in the Albion, they meet Matt's workmate, Sam Downes. Matt has formed a strong bond with Sam and they have ambitious plans for the future, potentially forming a partnership to go into business for themselves. On Sunday morning, Matt meets Ellen, Herb and May at the hotel and escorts the trio to church in the next street. St Matthews is a small church and it's crowded. Matt tells of plans to add a new wing to seat an additional 120 people. Ellen is not unduly impressed by the appearance of the saintly Collick, 'He is smaller than I expected and quite bald. Still, he conducts a dignified service and he preaches a good sermon.'

'The Boulder people regard him as a modern-day St Paul,' Matt says by way of reply. 'He raised funds to build a church and rectory, all within a year of his transfer to Boulder and he has also started a church school in a spare building on the Lake View mine lease. The school has grown to over 100 pupils and is still growing. In the evenings, he runs a boys' club and a men's club. He is a phenomenal worker and he is utterly selfless and generous with his time and what little money he has.'

After church they return to the hotel, where they are joined by Joseph after his Sunday sleep-in and walk eastwards to view the bristling poppet heads, steam, dust and clattering stamp batteries of the 'Golden Mile'. Joseph is curious about the plethora of chimneys emitting sulphurous fumes which are, to him, an unexpected feature of this iconic gold-mining centre. Matt has no ready explanation, 'All I know is, when the wind blows the smoke over Boulder, it makes your eyes sting and people start coughing. I will try to find out what they are doing before your next visit.'

After travelling by coach two miles to Kalgoorlie, they lunch at the prestigious Palace Hotel, built of brick and local stone, at the intersection of Hannan and Maritana Streets only two years previously. Ellen is captivated by the two-storey foyer, particularly the grand staircase, with its polished jarrah balustrade ascending to the upper floor. They spend the rest of the afternoon wandering up and down Hannan Street, taking in the many notable buildings. Amongst these, the government building housing the Warden's Court and Post Office is the most impressive, built of coffee-coloured local stone and surmounted by a high clock tower, rotunda and copper dome. Joseph is particularly taken by many of the hotels, the bold architecture of which outshines their counterparts in Coolgardie. He has already decided he needs to come back to find out more about the Golden Mile but now he relishes the idea of a 'pub crawl' taking in the Star and Garter, Kalgoorlie, York, Oriental, Palace, Australia, Exchange, Criterion and Federal Hotels, all on Hannan Street. Matt has noticed Ellen's favourable reaction to the staircase in the Palace and ushers the group into the York Hotel, where there is a less grandiose but still very ornate, staircase. Then they hear the distant strains of band music, so Matt guides them to Victoria Park where a brass band is playing, in a large rotunda topped by a pointed cupola, before a large audience. Their time is getting short to catch the train to Coolgardie so they walk quickly past avenues of exotic trees, fountains and flourishing bougainvillea trained over archways. Reaching the Kalgoorlie railway station, they are again struck by the warm mellow gold, pink and cream tones of the local stone used in its construction. After the bustle and sense of permanency of Kalgoorlie and

Boulder, they realise Coolgardie is falling behind in terms of progress and prosperity.

Joseph returns the following Sunday to undertake a guided tour of the Golden Mile with Dick Joyce, one of Matt's friends, who is a shift boss at the Great Boulder mill. Matt accompanies them to learn something about mining for himself. Dick tells them that a lot of the gold in the lodes of the Golden Mile is refractory and cannot be recovered by conventional methods. This problem was not apparent when the mines started treating weathered ore near the surface but when they reached the water table, recoveries dropped off drastically. It was found that much of the gold was so intimately mixed with sulphide minerals, such as pyrite and arsenopyrite, that amalgamation and cyanide extraction methods only recovered a fraction of the gold present. Some of the gold actually occurs as exotic telluride minerals, which are only known in a few localities around the world. The solution is to produce a sulphide concentrate, which is roasted in a furnace, driving off the sulphur as sulphur dioxide fumes. The residue or calcine, is then leached by cyanide. This is just the first step in a pretty complex process which results in satisfactory overall recoveries, underpinning the profits of the many local mining companies.

'So that's the reason for the toxic fumes we smell when the easterlies blow,' says Matt. Dick and Joseph nod in agreement.

'Of course, the difficulties experienced, at first, means plenty of gold went out with the 'slimes.' Those slime dumps south of Boulder will no doubt be worth re-treating many times as gold extraction methods improve,' adds Dick.

Joseph learns much more during his morning with Dick before thanking him and taking leave of the pair, apparently to go back to Coolgardie. In fact, he spends the afternoon sampling beer in a succession of the pubs in Hannan Street, before taking the train to Coolgardie. He has correctly surmised that Matt would be an unsatisfactory drinking partner, having been strongly influenced by his mother's abstemious views. When he returns to the Lindsay Street home in a jovial mood, Ellen serves dinner in silence, with a disapproving expression. Joseph is undeterred and repeats his Kalgoorlie expeditions frequently over the next few months. Only when Ellen insists on accompanying him to see Matt do his pub visits moderate.

With autumn, come cooler nights and mornings and extremely hot days become a rarity. One Sunday, while the family is at church, Joseph sets out to walk to the south of Coolgardie, hoping to learn about the mysterious practice of 'dry-blowing.' Joe has given him directions to the 'Empress of Coolgardie,' 'Just in Time' and 'Four in Hand' leases, south-west of Tindalls, where several practitioners of the art of dry-blowing are known to be working gold-bearing alluvium. It is a warm, still day and he relishes the prospect of a good walk in the bush and learning more about prospecting in terrain devoid of streams or lakes. South of the suburb of Montana, he strolls through pleasant eucalypt woodland until he sees and hears the mining activity at the Tindalls mining centre. Veering to the right he immediately sees two clouds of red-brown dust in the distance. Drawing closer to the first of these, he can discern a human figure in the centre of a blinding cloud of dust, standing beside a chest-high vibrating and rattling contraption. The man is operating levers with each hand which is causing the dust to billow around. Periodically, he stops working the levers, the dust settles and he shovels dirt from a pile behind him into the top of the contraption and a growing pile of dirt away from the base. Then he resumes working the levers again and the dust cloud forms anew. Joseph is intrigued by this novel scene and careful to stay out of the dust, remains unseen by the dry-blower until he stops to shovel once more. Joseph then steps into the line of sight of the digger, who immediately turns to meet the visitor. His head, hair, arms and clothes are covered in a thick layer of red-brown dust. Only the whites of his eyes shine brightly, in stark contrast to his drab appearance.

'I'm Jim Cruickshank, owner of this lease. Who are you and what is your business?'

'My name is Joseph Mazzucchelli. I have recently arrived in Coolgardie from Victoria and I am curious about dry-blowing. Would you please show me your machine and what it does?'

'Well, that's all right then,' Cruickshank says and proceeds to give Joseph a description of the process. Joseph sees that the contraption consists of an external frame holding a series of cascading sieves, which can be jiggled by a lever operated by the right hand. The left hand operates a modified bellows, which directs a jet of air upwards through the assembly of sieves, throwing the lighter dust particles up into the air and away. The apertures of the screens vary from coarse at the top to fine at the bottom. A sloping board with transverse riffles collects concentrate, hopefully containing gold particles, at the bottom. A pair of wheels at the base enables transportation of the device around the lease wherever new dirt is thought to merit treatment. Cruickshank is sufficiently trusting to pan some concentrate for Joseph. Several grains and flakes of fine gold are recovered.

'Of course, you occasionally pick up nuggets sitting on the screens,' he says. 'They are the really good days and when there is a bit of wind so the dust blows away, instead of all over you. This is a pretty good lease; I'm getting enough gold on top of my weekly wage from Bayley's Reward mine to live the good life and save for the future.'

Joseph has learned enough about dry-blowing to know it is not for him. At his age and financial status, he would prefer the sort of prospecting where you can pick up nuggets or lumps of quartz liberally laced with free gold, without too much exertion or getting too dirty. He also knows from personal experience that you need to be the first in on a new find to reap this kind of reward.

The Coolgardie International Exhibition opens in March 1899, with appropriate pomp and ceremony and runs until September. The original proposal by the Coolgardie Mine Managers' Institute was for a Mining Machinery Exhibition, to open in October 1897. The response by overseas machinery manufacturers persuaded the organisers to make it an International Mining and Industrial Exhibition and postpone the opening until 1898. It is intended to emulate previous International Exhibitions in London and Melbourne in celebrating progress in science, technology, culture and national or colonial achievement. There were several delays, firstly due to problems in shipping mining equipment from overseas and secondly due to a strike by lumpers in Fremantle. There had been a certain amount of bickering in the local press in the lead-up to the opening; the other colonies, apart from South Australia, had not contributed displays; local businesses were not sufficiently supportive and so on.

Past grievances are all forgotten when the Exhibition opens. The Coolgardie Miner proclaims the Exhibition is a *'Stupendous Undertaking…. Brought to a Successful Issue.'*

The opening ceremony is attended by 5,000 people. At the banquet following the opening ceremony, the Premier, Sir John Forrest, speaks of the achievement of those who had made a town like Coolgardie in a place which *'seven or eight years ago had been an arid wilderness, occupied by black-fellows and a very few kangaroos.'*

The captains of visiting naval ships from the USA and Austria are also guests at the banquet. The Austrian captain expresses his *'astonishment at seeing a town like Coolgardie in the centre of the desert. The lawns and fountains surrounding the (Exhibition) building defiantly celebrate the conquest over nature.'*

The editor of the Coolgardie Miner picks up this theme again in reporting that the Goldfields Water Scheme will be *'the ultimate triumph over the desert landscape.'* The development of the Goldfields, the Water Scheme and the Exhibition are *'all part of a lasting monument to the energy and inevitableness (sic) of the Anglo-Saxon race.'*

The Mazzucchelli family are among the early visitors to the Exhibition. The displays of magnificent gold nuggets and specimens from Coolgardie and surrounding areas attract most interest and acclaim. The centrepiece of the mining machinery display is a working stamp mill, which crushes parcels of prospector's ore free of charge. One of the biggest displays is the Agricultural Court, devoted to scientific advances in weed and pest control and research into varieties of produce suitable to the climate.

There are also separate courts promoting the York district, the south-west and an exhibit extolling the properties of Jarrah timber. Ellen makes a point of visiting the Women's Industrial Court, to which she has contributed a crocheted quilt. She does not win a prize but her work is mentioned in newspapers in Coolgardie, Kalgoorlie and Perth. The Coolgardie choir and orchestra entertain guests at the opening and the concert hall in the Pavilion is the venue for concerts throughout the duration of the Exhibition. Sporting events between teams and individuals from Goldfields towns also continue for six months.

Overall, 61,000 people attend the Exhibition over the six months it is open. Most of these are from Western Australia and there is some disappointment the Exhibition has failed to attract more interstate and international patronage. However, the Exhibition has convinced many Western Australians of the importance of the Goldfields to the State's economy and brought Goldfielders, previously thought to be mainly Victorians, together with the rest of the colony's population. This turns out to be an important factor in the forthcoming referendum on Federation. The WA Premier announces at the closing ceremony that the gold specimens will be exhibited at the 1900 Paris Exhibition and Glasgow in 1901. This will further confirm the WA Goldfields as one of the richest in the world. The rest of the exhibits are sold to recoup expenses and the Exhibition buildings will be used as a School of Mines.

The weather through the autumn months is fine and pleasant and apart from a few hot spells, marked by warm and sunny days, with crisp nights. Herb plays cricket for the St Andrew's second eleven. May joins the Cosmos Tennis and Croquet Club. Then it is winter.

The house is bitterly cold in winter when overnight temperatures frequently drop to zero and below. Thankfully, the wood fire in the kitchen stove keeps burning all day. This is where the family spends most of their time. In the evenings, Joseph and Ellen take prime position on comfortable chairs in front of the stove, while the children conduct their activities further back at the table at where most meals are eaten. The sun shines warmly from clear blue skies most days in winter and the family spends as much of the daytime as possible outdoors, whether working in the garden, attending functions in town or going for picnics in the nearby bush. On the rare overcast, windy or rainy days, they light a fire in the parlour and read, sing around the piano or play cards. After the winter rain, a vegetable patch is established and Ellen frequently mentions, with pride, when the evening meal includes home-grown turnips, peas or silverbeet. A lemon tree is planted and thrives on the contents of chamber pots which all members of the family use at night in preference to making the dark, cold trek out the back to the lavatory.

Spring comes early in 1899. A period of warm sunny days commences in mid-August and the family, including Selena, decides on a bush picnic on the first Sunday. Matt, with a newly grown moustache, makes the trip from Boulder to accompany them. Joseph and Ellen are surprised by the number of flowering plants, blues, yellows, pinks and the aromatic red-brown, waxy flowers of the native hop bush that had so impressed Joe in his early days. May makes the best botanical find, a solitary Sturt's Desert Pea, a ground-hugging creeper with clusters of vertical, pointed vivid red and black flowers. Spring in the desert is certainly not the drab affair they had expected.

After lunch, Matt makes a surprise announcement, he has been smitten by one Clara Christina Cronk and is intending to propose. Before he does so, he would like to bring her to Coolgardie to meet the other members of his family. All present agree they want to meet the girl that has taken their serious brother's fancy, as soon as possible. Ellen suggests Matt bring her for a home-cooked meal next Saturday night. Matt spends the next hour answering questions about Clara and her family. She is very young, not yet 17 and was born in Charters Towers in Queensland. Her father was a prospector and joined the gold rush in 1894. He had found enough gold at Kurnalpi, 45 miles north-east of Kalgoorlie, to establish a wine and spirit business at Kamballie, on the south-east extremity of Boulder. Ellen expresses alarm at this, 'I hope they are not big drinkers.'

'Not at all,' says Matt. 'They are good Anglican people and the shop sells general groceries and feed for animals. Wine and spirit are only part of the trade. Besides, Clara says her father was a famous professional athlete, known everywhere between Ballarat and Charters Towers as 'honest George Cronk.'

'I would like to meet her father and learn about his prospecting experiences,' says Joseph.

The family dinner the following Saturday with Clara passes off well enough. She is very pretty, with lots of curly auburn hair, huge mesmerising, almost hypnotic eyes, full lips and a tiny waist. She seems nervous to begin with but opens up when the other young women present, Maria, Lena and May, engage with her. After Matt and Clara depart to catch the late train back to Boulder, those left behind agree that Matt and she will make a good couple.

Matt proposes marriage almost immediately and is accepted. The wedding date is set for March 1901. A dinner is arranged in the Albion Hotel, Boulder, with the Cronk family. In the course of a very pleasant night, Ellen finds out that Harriet Cronk, George's wife, is the sister of the well-known Queensland politician, Charles McDonald. Joseph has a long conversation with George Cronk about prospecting and Matt and Clara feel satisfied with the rapport developing between the Mazzucchellis and Cronks. As Joseph and Ellen are staying the night, George suggests they visit George's business and home in Kamballie next day. By the time Joseph and Ellen catch the train to Coolgardie on Sunday afternoon, they have not only formed a warm relationship with the Cronks but also have a better appreciation of the size and vigour of Kalgoorlie and Boulder.

For Joseph and Ellen, Coolgardie and the Eastern Goldfields of Western Australia live up to the picture which had been painted by reports in Victorian newspapers and Joe's letters. There is the frequent excitement of new finds, periodic reports as to how developments are progressing at outlying locations such as Bonnie Vale, Goongarrie, Kunanalling, Norseman, Menzies, Leonora, Laverton and Widgiemooltha. The names of individual mines and leases have the familiar evocative romance as those in Stawell and New Zealand; The *Redemption* suggests atonement for past mistakes or unrewarded toil; *Happy Jack* perhaps describes the character of the owner; *Lady Charlotte* might be a tribute to the prospector's wife or prospective lover; *Big Blow* descriptive of a large outcrop of quartz; *Mystery Mint* optimistically foretells of a hidden fortune, etc. Not only is the town of Coolgardie developing apace but satellite towns in the surrounding district are springing up, making Coolgardie the hub of civilisation in what has been a trackless wilderness less than a decade previously. Even smaller towns such as Kunanalling, Bulong, Kanowna, Menzies, Leonora and Laverton all have their own hotels, breweries, newspapers and many are connected by railway with frequent services each day. The twin towns of Kalgoorlie and Boulder some 25 miles to the northeast are outstripping Coolgardie's development and are soon to boast a tram service. It was intended at the outset of the bold project to pipe water from the west coast to the Eastern Goldfields, that the scheme would end at a tank on Toorak Hill in Coolgardie. Due to the growing riches of the Golden Mile this changed during construction, to terminate the project in Kalgoorlie. The Goldfields towns will soon be able to establish parks and grassed sporting fields and citizens can contemplate gardens in their own homes producing fresh fruit, vegetables and flowers.

All manner of sport is pursued with vigour in Goldfields towns. Running and horse racing are popular, as is the new craze of cycling. The Westral Cycle Meeting, held on Boxing Day each year, attracts the best cyclists in the colony to Coolgardie. With many of the population coming from Victoria, their version of football is taken up as the main winter sport, while men of European origin prefer soccer. Cricket matches between Kalgoorlie and Coolgardie are so keenly contested the local papers refer to them as 'Test Matches'. Despite the scarcity and cost of water, swimming pools are built in both Coolgardie and Kalgoorlie and swimming contests between the towns are also hotly contested. May plays tennis at the Cosmos club in Coolgardie and is even reported to have played cricket for the victorious Coolgardie Ladies' team against the battery workers. Joe and Matt take up cycling, primarily as a means of getting around their respective towns but also as a recreational pursuit.

Politics are the subject of frequent public meetings and discussion in pubs and other informal venues. The proposal for a Federation of the six Australian colonies becomes a hot topic in the countdown to January 1901. There are many in Western Australia, mainly in the capital, Perth and agricultural south-west who are reluctant to join with the eastern colonies, fearing their isolation will not lead to a fair sharing of the benefits. The Goldfields are decisively in favour of Federation, much of the population having come from Victoria, New South Wales and Queensland. Meetings of the Amalgamated Certificated Engine Drivers' Association, which Joseph attends, are particularly fiery affairs at this time. A strong majority of the members demands the executive inform the Premier of Western Australia of their determination to join the Federation, even if Perth and the agricultural regions in the south-west of the State do not. The Premier, Sir John Forrest, makes the construction of a trans-continental railway from Adelaide to Kalgoorlie a condition for Western Australia's entry into the proposed federation.

Ellen's main interest outside the family is the church. She immerses herself in good works under the direction of the Venerable Barton Parkes. She attends Sunday and mid-week services, Mothers' Union meetings and Bible studies in private homes, cleans silverware, arranges flowers and enthusiastically embraces special projects like fetes and busy bees. As time goes on she becomes more antagonistic towards alcohol and Joseph's liking for a drink. She lectures her children on the evils of drink and nags Joseph.

The Goldfields as a whole, is a lively community. There is no shortage of entertainment. Theatres provide drama and burlesque. Music of every type thrives. Brass bands, of which there are several, give concerts in the rotunda in Central Park. They are particularly popular and are in demand for street parades, which are a regular feature to celebrate milestones or important events. None surpasses that which occurs on Saturday 19 May 1900, when news arrives of the Relief of Mafeking. This minor victory in the Boer War is widely celebrated throughout the British Empire. In Coolgardie, an impromptu street procession along Bayley Street and to the Exhibition Grounds is organised, replete with three brass bands followed by the Coolgardie Cadet Corps, police, both mounted and on foot, fire brigades, nurses and football teams, all in uniforms. A concert that evening is held in the quadrangle of the Pavilion raising £33 for the War Relief Fund. A public holiday is declared for the following Monday and celebrations continue with spontaneous singing of patriotic songs such as 'Soldiers of the Queen.'

Above all, Joseph and Ellen see the Goldfields as a close-knit, 'can-do' community. They are still astounded at the rapidity with which all the trappings of civilisation have been established in such a harsh, desert environment. They see mining, specifically gold mining, as the motivating force behind the achievement of so much, in so short a time.

In the same week as the Relief of Mafeking is celebrated, Joe marries Selena Rutherford in St Andrew's Church.

Marriage of Joe and Selena Mazucchelli. Coolgardie, May 1900. From left: Joseph, Albert, Ellen, May, Herb, Matt, Joe, Maria, Selena, Augustus (Alf) King.

The *Coolgardie Miner* reports the event in minute detail, including descriptions of the dresses worn by all the ladies in attendance and the gifts given by the parents of the newlyweds and exchanged by members of the wedding party.

The family poses for photographs outside Joe and Selena's house, all in formal dress and with serious expressions. The bride wears a white, lacy dress with a high frilled collar and a veil topped with a floral arrangement. The bridesmaids, Maria and May, wear wide-brimmed hats, Maria's at a rakish angle. Both have dark hair, May's long and Maria's bobbed. Ellen is hatless, in a dark dress, with short, dark hair parted in the middle. The Mazzucchelli men all wear bow ties and waistcoats under their jackets, with fob chains. Joseph, sitting to attention, has grey hair but black eyebrows and a prolific, droopy, black moustache. Joe strikes a more relaxed and confident pose. His moustache is dark, like his hair but turned up at the ends. The centrepiece of the photo is an arrangement of the wedding gifts; silverware, crystal, china, quilts, lamps and a clock, contrasting starkly with the backdrop of unpainted corrugated iron and the bare, gravelly earth of the yard in front.

The newly-weds depart on the night train to Kalgoorlie en route to Menzies, keen to familiarise themselves with another Goldfields town. They are surprised next day to find how different the country around Menzies and further north appears, compared to the Eastern Goldfields. Eucalyptus trees are restricted to the dry river-beds snaking through the countryside. The dominant trees are more diminutive drab varieties of mulga, a species of acacia. But on the ground is a riot of colour, pink, yellow and white everlastings and the occasional cluster of vivid, red Sturt's Desert Peas. These only appear in good seasons after rain, as this one is and the reason they decided to honeymoon here. They also learn that, unlike Coolgardie, the groundwater is fresh but so rich in dissolved minerals that soap refuses to lather when they wash.

Joseph increasingly spends his evenings sampling the numerous hotels and taverns. His rationale to Ellen is, it is essential to learn what is happening in their new town. To an extent he has already demonstrated this to be true. This is how he had learned of the vacancy for an engine driver at the Bayley's United mine, which he was able to secure but he is also gleaning much information on prospecting activities in and around Coolgardie. Many new gold discoveries are still being purchased by entrepreneurs and floated on the London Stock Exchange. European investors apparently have an insatiable appetite for Western Australian gold, despite the spectacular failure of some heavily promoted ventures, epitomised by the notorious 'Golden Hole' at Londonderry, 11 miles south of Coolgardie. This was a fabulously rich outcrop of gold-bearing quartz. A shallow shaft yielded so much gold that it was sealed off and guarded after its purchase by English investors, headed by the Earl of Fingall, while a company was floated to exploit the find. When reopened by the newly formed Londonderry Gold Mine Limited, it was found that virtually all the gold had already been mined and the hopeful shareholders lost the money they had invested.

Frequently, prospectors flush with funds from the sale of their leases, throw wild parties, replete with French champagne, to celebrate their new wealth. Joseph considers himself, at the age of 58, too old to engage in overly physical endeavours but he has capital to invest and is looking for an attractive opportunity. He is tempted to purchase shares in some of the companies being floated but finds it difficult to decide which are genuine prospects and which are duds. At the same time, it must be said, he enjoys drinking and chatting with other men, including, at times, his adult sons. In Joe's company, he meets several of the town's leading businessmen, including the owner of a real estate business. This man convinces Joseph of the merits of investment in several property assets. After all, the town is booming and clearly has a great future. Even investors from England are buying real estate in Coolgardie, so certain are they that it will become a major city.

From time to time, news comes of the doings of Matteo's family in Stawell. In the early summer of 1900, the whole family is assembled in the Lindsay Street house when the mail arrives. A letter from Margaret, Matteo's widow includes a cutting from the local paper, *The Stawell News and Pleasant Creek Chronicle*. When Joseph is reading the cutting, his face takes on an ashen hue and he becomes agitated.

'What's wrong?' Ellen queries. 'Something serious?'

Without saying a word, Joseph hands her the cutting and she too reads it with an increasingly worried expression.

'How disastrous, your cousin Stephen's house has burned down,' she says to the adult children when she finishes reading. She looks up and waves the slip of paper vaguely in the direction of Joe, Maria and Albert, who are sitting on the other side of the kitchen table. Joe reaches forward eagerly, snatches it and starts to read. As he reads, he makes peculiar snorting noises, trying, with limited success, to suppress the urge to laugh out loud.

'I know it is a serious matter,' he chuckles, 'but no-one was hurt and it is really quite funny. I think I'd better read it aloud for the rest of you,

'CONFLAGRATION IN PATRICK STREET

Captain Mazzuchelli's House Destroyed

A Bucket of Water Might Have Saved It

But the Tap Ran Dry

……….. a conflagration which took place in Patrick Street last evening at about nine o'clock, resulting in the total destruction of the residence of Captain Mazzuchelli of the Stawell Fire Brigade and all its contents. It appears that Mrs Mazzuchelli went into the back bedroom to arrange the bed for one of the children and left the lamp on a table while she returned to get the child. As she left the room Captain Mazzuchelli heard a noise as of something falling and on going to ascertain the cause he found the lamp had fallen on to the floor, from which flames were rising. He at once rushed to the tap to get a bucket of water but there was none available. Captain Mazzuchelli states that if he could have obtained a supply of water he could easily have extinguished the fire. None was obtainable, however and the flames quickly spread until the whole building was enveloped. The alarm was at once given by someone who had noticed the fire and the fire brigade lost no time in getting to the scene but they might as well have stopped away for all the good they could do. The water simply dribbled out of the nozzle and there was nothing for it but to let the fire burn itself out. Fortunately, there was a considerable space separating the adjoining houses or there is no knowing what might have *been the result in the absence of a supply of water. In a very short time, the house and all its contents were completely demolished, a couple of boxes being all that was saved.'*

At this, the room erupts into a mixture of mirth and sympathy, even Joseph allowing himself a brief smile.

'Bad enough having your home burn down but how embarrassing for the captain of the fire brigade, even though it wasn't his fault,' Maria says. 'I recall how proud Matteo's family was when Stephen was appointed Captain,' recalls Joe. 'Do you remember that picture of Stephen, the one of him wearing the shirt with butterfly collar, the jacket with braid epaulettes and the fancy cap. And even Stephen's wispy moustache which he thought added gravitas.'

'Nevertheless, I shall write to Margaret to express sympathy on behalf of us all,' concludes Ellen, looking around to make eye contact with all present in a way that said the fun is over.

11

The Last Foray - 1901

New Year's Day, 1901, a Tuesday, is proclaimed a holiday to celebrate Commonwealth Day, the day the six colonies join in Federation. Celebrations in the WA Goldfields are somewhat low key, given their role in ensuring Western Australia is included in the new nation of Australia. The day starts with services in all Coolgardie churches. In the afternoon, some 1,500 children from Coolgardie and surrounding towns as far away as Kunanalling converge on the Exhibition Building for a picnic tea and a fun sports event. Elections for the Federal Parliament are still to be held and campaigning by aspiring candidates is still in progress. Perhaps this, the uncertainty about the future trajectory of the Federal experiment and the summer heat or a combination of all three serve to subdue festivities.

In March 1901 Archdeacon Collick goes off to the Boer War as a chaplain to the British forces. A large crowd gathers at the railway station in Kalgoorlie to see him off, including many Aboriginals, to whom he has so endeared himself. A profound sense of loss is felt throughout the Goldfields. He never comes back to the Goldfields, returning to England at the end of the conflict.

Earlier in March, Matt and Clara are married by Archdeacon Collick in St Matthew's Church. A reception for 35 is held at the bride's home in Kamballie. It is a happy occasion and leaves both families basking in a feeling of euphoria.

Marriage of Matt and Clara Mazzuchelli, Boulder, March 1901. From left: Unknown, Clara, Matt, May.

Another bombshell falls one month later, Joseph's employment at the Bayley's United mine is terminated. Made redundant after only two years at the job. The reference provided by management refers to a 'temporary shortening of hands' and Joseph is not the only one to find himself out on the street. In fact, it is the start of the long decline which will eventually rob Coolgardie of its glitter and lead to its status as the most famous mining ghost town in Western Australia. It is found that the high grade gold near the surface and in shallow workings does not continue at depth. This is in stark contrast to the lode complex south of Kalgoorlie where the modest surface showings are changing to bonanza grades of gold the deeper the mines are sunk and look like continuing to the centre of the earth. The lode complex occupying a square mile which was formerly known as 'Brookman's sheep paddock' is now referred to as the 'Golden Mile.' Kalgoorlie and Boulder are expanding in size and prosperity while Coolgardie falters and shrinks. Joseph, at age 59, must reassess his options.

Joseph and Ellen derive a modest income from their rental properties, so there is no great urgency for Joseph to seek employment but from what he can learn, there are limited options for work, particularly for a man of his age. Initially, he busies himself with projects around the house, gardening and minor maintenance. There is little scope to improve the existing garden. The shortage of fresh water makes growing vegetables and fruit trees difficult, while roses and flowers are considered a luxury few can afford. The Goldfields Water Scheme, to pipe water from the well-watered west coast some 300 miles to the Eastern Goldfields, has been under construction since 1896. Although construction of a dam, pipeline and pumping stations has progressed, there are many who say it will never work and is an expensive waste of the vast sums borrowed by the colony. In the meantime, water for Coolgardie is supplied by a massive condenser erected by the government. This produces 100,000 gallons of fresh water each day from 120,000 gallons of salty groundwater, using 100 tons of wood to fire the boilers. However, the cost is such that it can only be used for human consumption and washing, precluding its use in gardens. Like most gardens in Coolgardie, Joseph's house features only hardy plants that can survive long periods without water, such as the peppercorn trees for shade, native shrubs and succulents. Joseph has attempted to supplement these with decoratively arranged rocks, particularly white quartz.

While Ellen is busy looking after the house and family and pursuing good works with the ladies of St Andrew's Church, Joseph soon becomes bored and reverts to his old habit of drinking with mates who are similarly unemployed, much to Ellen's disapproval. However, a plan is hatching in Joseph's brain. New finds are still made in the bush surrounding Coolgardie. The best place to learn about new gold finds is in the pubs of the town. If such news reaches him early enough, there would now be nothing to stop him acting on it and being one of the early birds that gets the worm. One of his drinking mates reminds him it is the second mouse that gets the cheese but this only serves to further encourage Joseph. He hasn't discussed this with Ellen because he suspects she will only try to dissuade him, arguing he is too old for the rigours of prospecting. There are a lot of pubs to cover. He normally frequents the Denver City or Victoria but over the next few days he visits others frequented by the prospecting community.

Sure enough, news does come in of a new find, at a place called Boondi. Details are scant but it seems a party of prospectors has come into town with sacks of coarse gold, including some large nuggets from a previously unknown area some 60 miles to the north-west. The rumours speak of a prominent hill of diorite a few miles west of a dry salt lake. The new gold find is presumably of the type Joseph hopes for, where a sharp-eyed fossicker can pick up slugs and nuggets by himself. Water supplies in the area are said to be limited but there is a known gnamma hole in the vicinity where some can be obtained.

To Joseph, this is the chance he has been waiting for. He decides to make the journey on foot rather than take a horse because of the shortage of water. He will cover the first 20 miles by the coach service, travelling northwards through the established mining outposts of Bonnie Vale and Kunanalling. He will then strike off through the bush in a north-westerly direction, skirting around an extensive area of dry salt lakes. He will only be able to carry enough water for two days so it will be important that he locates the Wongi gnamma hole during his second day. If he can pick up the prospectors' tracks he should be able to not only find the gnamma hole but also the new find.

Fossicking Afar

To his surprise, Ellen raises few objections to his plan. The reality is that she recognises his need for a project that will keep him out of the pub and out of the house. She puts together the basic food supplies he will need for four days and sends him on his way with admonitions to take care. There is no necessity to take risks. The family needs him more than more worldly goods. As he leaves she embraces him in a way that recalls their first passionate years as newly-weds.

A sense of elation sustains him throughout the early stages of his journey on the coach to Kunanalling. He is confident of the success of his venture. He recalls that period earlier in his life, when he first sensed that he knew where a virgin patch of alluvial gold existed and that he alone could reap the rewards from that knowledge. His success in New Zealand had been even sweeter. He had anticipated where the search on the west coast would trend and had used his mountaineering skills to steal a march on the competition. This is different because he does not know where his search will take him but he is just as sure that he is going to find gold and prosper from its discovery.

Joseph alights from the coach at the Northlander group of workings, to the north of Mt Burges and despite his burden, sets off at a good pace. He feels he is gliding over the track, carried along on a wave of optimism. The glossy leaves of the salmon gums glint in the bright sunshine as he progresses north-westerly. The waist-high saltbush flats he crosses between clusters of salmon gums look particularly lush. A flash of green and yellow surprises and delights him as hundreds of budgerigars zoom and swoop in and out of a clump of tea trees. He marvels anew as he skirts around a thicket of young gimlet saplings. As he strides along, he starts to think ahead to the outcome of his expedition. He will upgrade the family home to ensure he and Ellen live in comfort for the rest of their lives. More important in his mind, are the accolades and respect he can expect from his peers. To show the world he is still able to succeed as a prospector at his advanced age is more important in his mind than monetary rewards.

He stops for lunch in the shade of a fine old gum tree, close by a thicket of gimlet saplings. Young eucalypt trees always appear so vigorous to him, despite the baking dry climate. He lunches well, on the corned beef sandwich Ellen has prepared for him, followed by a crisp and juicy green apple, all washed down with sweet black tea. The meal and his surroundings increase his feeling of satisfaction and peace with the world. A group of pink and grey galahs adorn every limb of a dead tree, flying off with a cacophony of squawks as he passes by. He makes a further 10 miles along what he takes to be the track to the gnamma hole before camping amongst rounded boulders of granite. He devours a good meal of corned beef, biscuits, tea and dried fruit and then settles into his blanket and gazes up at the brilliant display of stars until sleep overcomes him. It is a cool night, so he is ready to resume walking at daybreak, to get warm. He delays eating until mid-morning, by which time he estimates he has travelled another 10 miles.

During the afternoon, the wind changes around from the south-east to the north and it becomes noticeably warmer. The sky is streaked with wispy clouds and a gusty, hot wind is blowing. His thoughts as he hurries forward are, for the first time, assailed by some doubts. There are more intersecting tracks than he had anticipated. What if he takes a wrong turn and becomes lost before he can replenish his dwindling water supply? How long will this heatwave last? He knows he is not good in hot weather. His mouth will become dry, his lips will crack, his head will ache and he will feel weak.

By evening, his worst fears are realised. He should have reached water by now but he has not seen the indications which he has been looking for. The hot north wind is getting stronger, indicating an even hotter day is likely tomorrow. He makes camp in scrubby country, having no energy to look for a more pleasant situation. He has a good meal, devouring half of the remaining biscuits, corned beef and raisins, along with sweet tea but does not enjoy it. Only a little water is left in his water bag. If he does not find water early next day he fears doing 'a perish.' As he lies on top of his blanket, still sweating from the heat, he takes no pleasure from the stellar display above. He falls into a restless, troubled sleep.

He is wakened at dawn by the mournful cawing of a pair of crows. His lips are dry and cracked and his tongue is sticking to the roof of his mouth. He allows himself two mouthfuls of water and realises he barely has the same amount left in his water bag. The day passes in a haze. It is stupendously hot and he seems trapped in a maze of tracks that lead him back to the same place time and again. He is too weary to defend his eyes, ears and nostrils against the swarms of flies that try to invade his every orifice. Late in the afternoon, the sky becomes cloudy and the added humidity makes the heat even more oppressive. When night falls, he attempts to eat the rest of his corned beef but his mouth is so dry he can barely swallow. He manages only with the help of the last of his water. As he lies down to sleep the sky is lit up by flashes of lightning. There is no accompanying thunder and he surmises that any storm activity is far away. His fitful sleep is punctuated by nightmares. When morning comes, he is just sufficiently refreshed to realise he must abandon any thoughts of easy gold and focus on his own survival. He is already dehydrated and cannot count on finding any water on his trek. He reasons the safest and shortest route to salvation will be to go south and hope to reach the railway line or the road between Southern Cross and Coolgardie. There are daily trains, coaches and drays and help will almost certainly find him quickly. Even so he will have to walk for more than a day, possibly two days, in extreme temperatures, without water. He manages to get a fistful of raisins down before setting off in a southerly direction, leaving his blanket, prospecting tools, flour and tea behind.

It is another cloudy day and a hot wind is still blowing from the arid centre of the continent to the north-east. Despite the clouds, the sun bears down, adding to the furnace-like situation. The landscape through which he is now trudging is the most alien he has yet experienced. No blade of grass or living shrub relieves the baked, brick-red laterite plain that he is traversing. There are no living trees to provide shade. The sunlight is blinding and the heat seems to press down on him. Oh, for a cool, dark mine shaft he could descend to escape this heat! As he blunders on, the oven-hot air takes on an increasingly foul smell. Something or someone has died here. A smattering of dead mulga trees dot the flat expanse as far as he can see. The stark bleached trunks and pointed branches of the dead mulgas seem like bleached bones protruding from seared, tortured flesh. As the smell of death becomes more intense he comes across a dead kangaroo. It has been dead a long time. Its withered skin has shrunk back, exposing the bleached bones of its rib cage, powerful legs and bare skull. As he stumbles over ironstone rocks and weaves between the searching points of the horrible mulgas seeking to escape this foul-smelling plume, he shudders to think that he might soon fall down and blend into this landscape of death and desolation.

Now he is feeling faint and almost unconscious. He sits down, propped up against the trunk of a dead mulga tree. He tells himself he will rest a while and continue his journey when he feels stronger. An hour passes but he feels unable to raise himself. Rather, he feels sleepy and thinks he will lie down a bit longer. He falls into a restless sleep, more like a stupor, assailed by nightmarish dreams. While he lies there, oblivious to his surroundings, the clouds above gather into a black mass and a thunderstorm develops. Initially, a gusty wind whips up an intense dust storm which sweeps across the terrain. Then forks of lightning light up the gloom and thunder claps rumble and crash above the roar of the wind. All this merges with Joseph's troubled dreams. It isn't until a downpour of cold rain drenches him that he revives. For a moment he lies on his back with his mouth open, letting the rain moisten his lips and tongue. Hurriedly, he gets up and looks for ways to secure a supply of water for his onward journey.

Fortunately, he has kept his empty canvas water bag when he had dumped his prospecting gear. As the heavy rain continues, he finds small pools of water are collecting in the irregularities on the ironstone rock surface and he can scoop a small quantity into the bag. He drinks as much as he can and sets out, slightly revived, on his southward course. For a moment he contemplates retracing his steps and resuming his golden quest. Sanity prevails. He has nearly perished. He has no need for wealth or fame. His greatest urge is to be reunited with Ellen and his family

Presently, he becomes aware not all the trees are dead. There is not much difference. A few grey-green leaves adhere here and there to the upper branches. The ground slopes downwards ever so slightly and visibility diminishes as he is now walking through a grey-green smattering of living, head-high mulga trees.

After lurching onwards for another ten minutes, he emerges at the lip of a huge amphitheatre opening out at his feet. Curving away in a great arc to the east and west is a continuous line of cliffs, coloured an orange-brown at the top, grading to white clay at the base; what he has heard is called a breakaway. In softer white rock, immediately below the lip, are numerous shallow caves and even as he watches, their occupants, muscular grey and red-brown kangaroos, scatter in panic at the clattering stones he has dislodged in his stumbling approach. The lower slopes are littered with huge ironstone boulders, obviously collapsed by weathering of the cliffs. Splashes of turquoise green, contrasting with the ochre and cream colours of the cliffs are caused by distinctive native pine trees, which stud the escarpment. At the base of the slope, fresh water is trickling in ribbon-like stream-beds snaking away towards a distant salt-encrusted dry lake, gleaming on the horizon.

Although the ironstone escarpment is less than 30 feet higher than the plain below, the overall flatness of the terrain is such that he can see everything lying to the south-west for a distance of some 25 miles. As the unexpected grandeur of the scene slowly registers on his dazed consciousness, he suddenly remembers he is starving and still facing a thirsty death. Food, in the highly nutritious form of kangaroo meat is retreating from him at speed he can't match. He has frightened some of the kangaroos in his immediate vicinity but there might be others. He selects two rocks, large enough to inflict damage but small enough to be thrown and stealthily works along the escarpment to the south. As he goes, more kangaroos bolt from caves immediately below him, none offering the chance of a hit. He is just about to despair when a straggler emerges just below him. It scrambles to its feet, seemingly unsure as to whether to join the exodus of its fellows or not. It is just the chance Joseph needs. He lifts his biggest rock high above his head and hurls it down with both hands in the direction of his prey, scoring a direct hit about the left haunch. He has clearly broken a leg bone, immobilising the small marsupial and it is a simple matter to descend the scarp and administer the coup de grace with a stick.

While the haunches of his kill lie across an open fire cooking, Joseph sets about following the criss-crossing tracks made by the kangaroos which bolted from the breakaway caves. The tracks converge onto a well-marked trail which he hopes will lead to water and sure enough, after some 500 yards he comes across a soak in the headwaters of a sandy creek. Animals have clearly been digging in the damp sand to obtain water and he finds that excavation of a small hole is rewarded by a trickle of clear, albeit somewhat brackish water. He stays there a long time, slaking his thirst. By deepening his excavation, he can fill his water bag. When he returns to his fire by the escarpment, he eats the kangaroo meat until sated, putting the remainder of the cooked meat in his pack. It is very tough meat and his jaws ache from the chewing but his hunger is satisfied and he feels his strength returning. By this time, it is dark. He stretches out and settles down for another night under the stars.

It is a cold night without his blanket and he rises at first light to resume his trek. He again climbs the escarpment and scours the horizon for signs of civilisation. There is little besides the white salt lake immediately to the south, after which a uniform sea of grey-green vegetation, punctuated by occasional low hills, extends to the horizon. A number of vertical columns of dust can be seen in different quarters but these he identifies as willy-willies, mini tornadoes which are ever-present in the hot desert. One puff of dust, far to the south-east, appears less cylindrical in shape and he thinks he can almost make out a break in the tree-line below it. Could he be seeing the head frame of a mine or some other construction? He decides he has nothing to lose by walking in that direction and finding out. In any case, if he keeps walking in a southerly direction, he will eventually intersect a road or railway line.

He gathers his pack and sets off in the direction of his target, stopping once more at the soak to drink and refill his waterbag. He is again in high spirits. Despite the failure of his prospecting venture, he feels confident he can reach the railway line between Southern Cross and Coolgardie and help.

He is still in a buoyant mood when he reaches the edge of the salt lake. He estimates it to be some two miles across and the surface appears dry, firm and dead flat. Without a second thought, he sets off at a cracking pace to the southeast, making the most of the firm, flat going. Heat reflected off the white salt crust causes the appearance of pools of water ahead but he surmises these are only mirages. In less than an hour, the trees on the far side of the lake are coming into clear focus and he is congratulating himself on his excellent progress, when he first notices a change in the surface he is walking on. In place of the hard, white salt crust is moist brown clay, which is somewhat slippery. Looking ahead, it seems the pools of water he could see were not mirages but are indeed real. It might only be inches deep so he presses on. By the time he has covered another 50 yards, his boots are sinking into the surface. With each step, more mud is clinging to his boots and he realises he will soon be floundering in an intractable bog. At the same time a cloud of mosquitoes descends on him. He is driven mad by the whining sound of them crowding around his head. They are undeterred by his flailing arms and alight on any exposed skin. He slaps at them on his hands and arms, his neck, ears and cheeks. Their squashed bodies lie in blotches of the blood they have sucked from him. He hurriedly looks to both sides and decides the salt crust looks more continuous to the east.

Joseph retraces his steps until he is on dry salt again and after scraping the heavy coating of mud off his boots, he can resume a steady walking pace in an easterly direction. As he gathers momentum, he leaves most of the mosquitoes behind. An hour later, it seems he can make his way southwards to the southern margin of the lake on dry salt. As it turns out he must deviate to the east again and it is another two hours, after a series of dog-leg detours, that he is finally able to reach the trees on the southern margin of the lake. The storm on the previous night and the northerly wind have shifted the scant moisture on the surface of the lake to the southern side, forming a barrier to his progress.

Now Joseph has crossed the lake, he has lost his bearings with respect to the patch he has been heading for. However, he knows he has made progress towards his ultimate destination, Coolgardie. He still has food and water, so he isn't unduly worried but he feels tired and weak. He changes his bearing to south and walks on through typical pleasant eucalypt woodland, which lifts his spirits. It is a cool, sunny day and his thoughts again turn towards gold. Ever since the thunderstorm, he has been in completely trackless country. His southerly path takes him towards a low rise and he deviates a little to the west to reach the highest point. He cannot see his original target from this point but notes the next hill to the south-west is somewhat higher. At the summit of the second hill, outcrops of diorite confirm his view that he is in an area where gold might be found.

What he needs is to find some quartz veining. Forgetting his original objective, the patch where he had sighted dust and possibly human activity, he starts circling around looking for tell-tale signs that might lead to gold. On the western flank of this hill, the dioritic rocks are broken into slivers standing on end, before disappearing under soil.

Looking over the soil-covered valley towards the next hill to the west, which is clearly granite, he thinks he sees a scatter of white quartz pebbles. With growing excitement, he hurries to the spot, only to find what he had thought to be quartz, is in fact nodules of caliche, found commonly in desert soils. Disappointed, he retraces his steps to the hilltop and scans the horizon for signs of human activity. He sees a possible clearing which could be the place he had seen from the breakaway but it is too far away to reach in what remains of the day. He decides to continue prospecting around this location for the rest of the day but first thing in the morning he must set out for civilisation, whether he finds gold or not. For two hours, while the daylight lasts, he wanders the undulating diorite terrain looking for his Eldorado, to no avail.

Next morning, Joseph eats the last of his food and sets off in the direction of the clearing, expecting at least a 12 mile walk and much more if his objective turns out not to be a place of human activity. As he walks, he mulls over his disappointment at not finding any sign of gold in such a promising and clearly untouched patch of prospective rocks. About two miles into his journey, he crosses diagonally, a well-incised dry watercourse. Scattered along its bed of greenstone rock are cobbles of quartz. He surmises the creek probably rises amongst the hilly diorite country he had just come from but further to the east than he was able to prospect before darkness had curtailed his search. Knowing he cannot afford to deviate from his homewards push, he decides he should at least have a closer look at the quartz. Lacking his prospecting tools, he resorts to breaking the quartz cobbles by banging them together. The fresh surfaces now exposed excite him. The quartz is white and partly translucent, seamed with thin dark mineral bands. He recalls miners talking of laminated quartz from the gold deposits at Norseman, some 100 miles south of Coolgardie but try as he might, he can't see gold. He resumes his trek to the south, absent-mindedly putting one of the more attractive of the laminated quartz cobbles in his pocket. His thoughts again turn to his survival. He has averted disaster once on this trip. His hopes now rest on reaching some outpost of civilisation before what little remains of his water is exhausted. He is also getting hungry and, above all, anxious to be back with his family.

Again, walking through eucalypt woodland, Joseph makes steady progress through the morning while it is cool. It is a still day and becomes hotter in the afternoon and his pace flags accordingly. He allows himself a mouthful of water every now and then but dark thoughts again start to nag him. He is visualising himself dying of thirst under the roasting sun when he realises he has just walked over something quite alien. He turns and sees what he has almost failed to notice, the Perth to Kalgoorlie railway line. He realises with elation that he is going to live. All he must do is follow the rail to the nearest siding. Even if he is unable to reach a siding, he will be able to flag down one of the several trains which pass every day.

Looking along the railway to east and west, he is unable to see any sign of a siding but he notices dust arising from a point slightly south of the line of the track, to the east. Although he is almost spent, he decides to walk in that direction, reasoning it will take him closer to his ultimate destination, Coolgardie and home. As he walks, the dust continues to rise and swirl from the same area and he becomes more confident of finding help. An hour before sunset, he pauses to listen and thinks he can hear machinery and general clatter. There is a bend in the railway half a mile ahead and he quickens his pace to reach it before nightfall. When he rounds the bend, a welcome sight greets his eyes. It is a construction site for one of the pumping stations which is part of the Goldfields Water

Supply. He can see men and horses, probably getting ready to quit for the night. He shuffles into the midst of the activity, unaware of the sight he presents; a sunburnt, dirty and unkempt wreck of a man. He can barely speak for exhaustion, mingled with relief, but the men sense his needs and he is soon sitting down with a steaming cup of tea. After this, the questions start.

'Where have you come from?' asks Fred, who seems to be the boss.

At first, Joseph thinks they have picked up his still distinct Italian accent, so he answers, as is his custom, 'Switzerland.' Then realises they want to know about his most recent journey. 'I live in Coolgardie but I've been prospecting to the northwest of here. I was lost and run out of water twice. I thought I was 'done for.' He tells them about his ordeal but stresses he has found nothing of interest. This is not quite true because he is already planning another trip to prospect the source of the laminated quartz and the greenstone country he traversed earlier today but he doesn't want others to know.

'You're twice lucky,' says Fred. 'Lucky not to perish and lucky to be here because a train will be here in half an hour to take us all into Coolgardie for the night. You'll be home in two hours.'

Joseph cleans himself up as best he can before the train comes, so as not to give Ellen and the family too big a fright. When he knocks on the door of the Lindsay Street house later that night, it is opened by Joe. 'Thank God, it's you,' he said. 'Mother was sure you were in trouble and called us all together to discuss what we could do about it. We were in a quandary. We didn't know where to start. Come and put us all out of our misery.'

Joe leads Joseph into the kitchen, where Ellen and all the children, apart from Matt, sit around the table. They all leap up with cries of joy. Ellen wraps herself around Joseph for a long time, followed by Maria, May and even the boys embrace him in their turn. Joseph, overcome with emotion, sits down, openly weeping. He is so thankful to be with his family again, he decides he will never spend another night away.

He soon regains his composure. Whilst consuming some bread and cheese, followed by some of Ellen's home-cooked cake, he relates the story of his adventure to the family. By the time he finishes, it is late and the family disperses to their homes. As he gets into bed with Ellen, she says, 'I think you are too old to go fossicking in the bush. I don't want to have to worry about you again, like I have these last few days.'

By way of answer, he tries to snuggle up close to her but she turns her back on him. 'You need a good long bath before you'll get a cuddle from me,' she snaps. 'Good night!'

12

Redemption - 1902 to 1909

After his return from the abortive prospecting trip, Joseph lies low for a time, thankful for the comforts of home after so nearly perishing. From time to time, his thoughts return to the prospective area he traversed on the last day of his misadventure. It would be easy to retrace his steps by train and foot to look for the source of the laminated quartz floaters he had seen in the dry creek bed. However, he thinks he will wait a while before he sets off again. Ellen is displaying a warmth towards him that he has not experienced for years. When they walk together they revive their old practice of holding hands. In bed at night and especially in the mornings, they are content to lie together in a close embrace for long periods. It makes Joseph reluctant to risk breaking the spell by going away again, so he puts thoughts of more prospecting to the back of his mind.

After a month or so, while Ellen attends a Mothers' Union meeting at the church, he makes his way to the Denver City Hotel in Bayley Street. His old friends are there as always, propped up on stools at the public bar. They welcome Joseph and he imperceptibly slips into his old habit of a daily session at the pub. The old-timers take turns in buying rounds of drinks and telling stories. They are the same stories every day but no one seems to mind or at least, no one objects. Joseph tells how Jake Francis left him in the lurch at the bottom of a dangerous shaft, how the Captain of the Stawell fire brigade's house came to burn down and even his encounters with the Reverend Ernest Brenton. He feels a bit sheepish talking about his failed prospecting ventures, including the Hanoverian Reef but his companions downplay his concerns. 'You can't always win but good on you for having a go,' is the attitude taken by the group.

On the home front, the activities of his family become more important than his own.

His children are faring well and he has become a grandfather, Joe's and Matt's wives having given birth to a boy and girl, respectively. Herb leaves Coolgardie to set up his own barbershop in the town of Malcolm, 135 miles north of Kalgoorlie. A railway line is under construction from Menzies to the gold-mining towns of Leonora and Laverton, in the Mt Margaret Goldfield. Malcolm is a busy junction between the two and services small mines in the surrounding area. In typical fashion, Herb throws himself wholeheartedly into the Malcolm community, playing football for Malcolm against neighbouring gold centres such as Mertondale and Kookynie. At the grand opening of the completed railway in 1902, he competes in handicap foot-races.

At the celebration to mark the baptism of Cecil, Joseph asks Joe, 'How is your business going?'

Joe says, 'The newsagency and stationery business is doing well, even though the earnings of the Coolgardie mines seem to be going down.'

'I suppose you're not sorry you decided to opt for a business career, instead of direct involvement in prospecting and mining,' Joseph conjectures, beer in hand.

'No, not at all,' says Joe. 'You went out every day in work clothes and came home every night covered in dirt. I can at least wear decent clothes while I earn my living.'

'That may be so but I think you are missing out on the fun and excitement of mining.'

'I don't think that is the case. I am in tune with the ups and downs of this mining town and I am amongst the first to hear of new developments and finds. I put you in the know about the Boondi find, didn't I? Even though it didn't go that well for you,' Joe adds.

'The less said about that the better,' says Joseph.

'Anyway, I do get involved in the mining game, I have started grubstaking a few prospectors and miners. It doesn't cost much, a few pounds per man per week but if they strike it lucky, I'll get a good share of the proceeds,' says Joe.

'You need to be careful,' says Joseph. 'There are a good many rascals amongst the mining set and you might not have the knowledge to know if they are cheating you. Even good men, when they get the gold lust, can be tempted to cheat. Anyway, I can see how you are regarded in this community and am very proud of you.'

1902 is also a notable year for the tragic suicide of the visionary State Engineer, Charles Yelverton O'Connor. O'Connor is the mastermind of the ambitious Goldfields Water Supply project and other major projects such as the harbour at Fremantle. The colony's government has committed a sum equivalent to its normal annual budget to the success of this project. O'Connor has many detractors in the Western Australian Parliament and press, who express doubts as to the scheme's success. In a fit of depression, O'Connor rides his horse into the waters of Cockburn Sound and shoots himself.

By the end of the same year, water flows through the pipeline into a huge tank on Toorak Hill, Coolgardie. The

Coolgardie Mayor's wife is the first to taste the water, drinking from a solid gold cup. The water is brown in appearance, presumably from dirt and rust in the pipeline and probably tastes less than ideal but that doesn't detract from the euphoria created by this long-awaited day.

The official opening of the Goldfields Water Supply Scheme occurs at both Coolgardie and Kalgoorlie on 24th January 1903, in the presence of Sir John Forrest and other dignitaries from the Commonwealth Government. When construction of the Scheme started in 1896, it was intended for the pipeline to terminate at Coolgardie. During construction, however, it becomes apparent that Coolgardie is declining, whilst Kalgoorlie is booming, so the pipeline is extended to Kalgoorlie.

As clear, pure water flows into the Mt Charlotte reservoir in Kalgoorlie, Forrest says, 'Future generations, I am quite certain will think of us and bless us for our far-seeing patriotism and it will be said of us, as Isaiah said of old, "they made a way in the wilderness and rivers in the desert."'

Herb leaves Malcolm in February 1903. The community organises a send-off for him in Hill's Hotel, attended by about 35 friends. Many toasts are proposed and responded to. A gold locket is presented to him in recognition of his many good qualities. The evening ends with singing and recitations. He then passes through Coolgardie en route to York, where he establishes a business, again as a barber and tobacconist. Later that year he marries an Adelaide girl, Olive Hey, in the Wesleyan church at York. He had met Olive in Kalgoorlie, where she had come from Adelaide in 1901, to help her sister with the birth of her first child.

Marriage of Herb and Olive Mazzucchelli, York, September 1903.

Also in 1903, Matt and his friend Sam take control of the Manhire Jewellery and Watchmakers business in Lane Street, Boulder, under the name of Mazzucchelli and Downes. When the signage of the shop changes, the new proprietors and their staff pose under the veranda outside. Matt is the tallest, wearing a dark suit and tie, with chains across his waistcoat. The other three are in shirtsleeves, presumably having come from work-benches inside.

Mazzucchelli & Downes, Lane Street, Boulder 1903.

The signage is extensive, white lettering painted on a black background. Every available surface carries a message:

'WATCHES & JEWELLERY SKILLFULLY REPAIRED'

'MAZZUCCHELLI & DOWNES, WATCHMAKERS & MANUFACTURING JEWELLERS'

'WATCHES, CLOCKS & JEWELLERY REPAIRED'

'YOUR OWN GOLD MANUFACTURED TO ANY DESIGN'

… with lots of artistic flourishes and an illustration of a popular type of gold brooch.

After the opening, which Ellen and Joseph attend, a celebration takes place at Matt and Clara's corrugated iron home in Wittenoom Street, Boulder. Matt regales Joseph with his vision for the partnership, 'It is the foremost business of its type in Boulder and is known for the highest quality goods and service. We intend to keep it that way. We think there is potential to make it even better. The tram network is under construction linking the main centres of Kalgoorlie and Boulder and the Boulder terminus will be right outside our shop. People coming from Kalgoorlie will soon be getting off the trams at our door. The whole tram service will run to times taken from the Mazzucchelli and Downes clock. It's the only big clock in Boulder.'

'Do you have any plans for direct involvement in mining ventures?' asks Joseph.

'No, we don't think that would be advisable. We know that in a rich mining centre like Boulder, there will always be a few people tempted to steal gold from the mines. Mr Manhire has been aware of a few suspicious characters offering to sell gold to him and he won't have a bar of it. We will be careful to guard our good name. We have plans to expand throughout Western Australia. We are not interested in short-terms gains that could tarnish our reputation.'

In 1904, Joe approaches Joseph with a proposition.

'My partner in Stawell wants to retire and has offered to sell me his share of the business. The trouble is, it's worth 500 pounds and I can't raise that amount at short notice. It occurred to me you might be interested in it as an investment.'

It is subsequently reported in the local press that Mr Joseph Mazzucchelli has paid 500 pounds for the stock and goodwill of The Arcade Stationery and Newsagency.

The main family event in 1904, is the marriage of Maria to Augustus Lismore (Alf') King. Alf has doted on Maria since Joe and Selena's wedding where he and Maria served as best man and bridesmaid.

About this time, Joseph's nephew, Matthew Ernest Mazzuchelli, is transferred by his employer in Ballarat to Sandstone, some 250 miles north of Coolgardie, to work in a newly acquired gold mine. Matthew, Matteo's youngest son, graduated as a metallurgist from the Ballarat School of Mines and then worked in the processing of gold ore from Ballarat mines. Matthew travels with his wife, Monica and infant daughter Mary Gertrude ('Tru'). The family rapidly become integral members of the Black Range and Sandstone community. Matthew plays football for the Sandstone team. Monica gives birth to two sons in Sandstone and Mary Tru starts at the convent school. Towards the end of World War I, the company winds up its operations in Sandstone and Matthew takes up farming at Dindiloa, east of Geraldton and later, Balla Balla. Monica gives birth to two more daughters. Tru becomes Sister de Lourdes of the Presentation Sisters order, later working in education throughout the Murchison and Mid-West. Joseph and Matthew's families remain in contact for many years.

Joseph takes quiet pleasure in the expansion of his family over the next few years as his tally of grandchildren grows to ten by 1908. While Ellen concentrates on instilling Christianity and good manners in the younger generation, Joseph accepts with delight any and all behaviour of his grandchildren, whenever possible. The family is plunged into grief in 1905 when Joe's third son, Ernest, becomes ill and dies at the age of only four.

Over the next few years, Joseph maintains a retiring disposition, while, in contrast, the public profile of three of his sons grows.

Joe finds various ways to get publicity for his business. One of the most cost-effective, is to pass on the latest editions of popular illustrated magazines from England, *Strand*, *Pearson's* and *London,* for review in the local newspapers. In 1905, Joe's business is appointed sole agent for *The Coolgardie Miner* and later, *The West Australian*. His is a prominent voice in public meetings and from 1907 onwards, he features in reports of the activities of the Coolgardie Chamber of Commerce and Industry on issues such as trading hours, street lighting, electricity charges and the fire brigade. He is also a vocal participant at shareholder meetings of the Coolgardie Mining, Development and Prospecting Company, which is struggling for financial support to develop the *Undaunted* gold mine at Menzies. He sits as part of a three-man Coroner's Jury looking into a suspicious fire which has destroyed the Mt Burges Hotel at Bonnie Vale and becomes Secretary of the Coolgardie Cemetery Board in 1909.

Matt's profile in Boulder follows a similar rising trajectory. He and his partner, Sam Downes, are appointed official time-keepers for the Boulder Cycle Club. Mazzucchelli and Downes receive publicity for donating medals and prizes for diverse sporting events; football, boxing, school athletic and Combined Friendly Societies Carnivals. Matt is also a Coroner's juryman, hearing cases such as mine fatalities and a salacious murder/suicide. He, at times, serves as a vestryman at St Matthew's Church and on the Boulder City Council. Like Joe, he manages to have the local paper print advertisements for the goods and services on offer from Mazzucchelli and Downes in the guise of news articles.

Both Matt and Joe become active Freemasons, taking on official roles in Boulder and Coolgardie.

Herb is no slouch in his new wheatbelt community. Herb realises his ambition to go farming when granted a parcel of 400 acres in the Dulbelling area, 30 miles from York, under Sir James Mitchell's Conditional Purchase Scheme in 1906. He adds a further 533 acres to the property, which he names Hampton Meadows. Over the next two years he continues to operate his barber and tobacconist business in York while building a house on the farm. Elected to the York Shire Council in 1907, he begins a lifetime as a vocal and constructive participant in local government affairs. Herb's wife, Olive, gives birth successively to five daughters, Muriel, Lois, Doreen, Mavis and Eva.

In 1907, when a thunderstorm floods the underground workings of the Westralia Mine in Bonnie Vale, six miles north of Coolgardie, Joe leaves his wife and son in charge of the shop and rides his bicycle to the site to offer help. This incident turns into a protracted rescue effort, when it is realised one miner, Modesto Varischetti, is trapped underground. Frantic efforts to pump the water out are proceeding too slowly so, in a bold initiative, a team of deep-sea divers are brought in from Perth. Five days after the mine flooded, a diver reaches Varischetti in an air pocket at the end of a rise and finds him still alive. Varischetti is supplied by the divers with food, candles and letters of encouragement. Varischetti writes letters back, saying farewell to his relatives and friends and thanking all concerned for the efforts on his behalf. Four days later, the water level has dropped sufficiently to bring him to the surface. The whole world, which has been following this drama, heaves a sigh of relief.

May becomes engaged to Norman Burrows, an accountant and plans for a wedding in 1908. At the engagement party, Joseph is approached by the father of his prospective son-in-law, Robert Burrows, with the offer of a job as an engine driver on the Redemption mine, just to the east of the town. Burrows, a lawyer, is a director and prime mover of the Coolgardie Redemption Gold Mining Company, which was floated in 1907. The Redemption Mine has had a chequered history. It was a high grade producer in the early days of the field and source of some incredibly rich gold specimens which contributed to the worldwide fame of Coolgardie. The previous owners of the mine had experienced problems due to flooding of the mine and had gone into debt. The main creditor is the lease owner, who had lent 5,000 pounds to pay debts and purchase machinery. Bankruptcy proceedings resulted in forfeiture of the mine and equipment.

Burrows joins with a number of investors from Coolgardie and Kalgoorlie putting out a prospectus to raise finance to purchase the mine and discharge existing debts. The prospectus includes testimony by the previous underground superintendent that 'it was a good mine but very badly managed.' He asserts, 'if a new shaft is sunk to 400 feet, with efficient pumping gear that a really good mine would be opened up which would prove worthy of the name Coolgardie Redemption.' The prospectus also includes a letter from the Secretary of the Mines Department, quoting the Minister for Mines as agreeing, 'if the concern were formed into a public company, with enough money raised to pay off present liabilities and to provide for an adequate pumping outfit and some dead work, an application for assistance for purchasing the pumping machinery might favourably be considered.' Shares in the company are largely taken up by loyal Coolgardie residents, like Joe, keen to arrest the decline of the town. A bitter letter is written to the *Coolgardie Miner* by the previous owner, disputing the assertion of his former superintendent in the prospectus about bad management and blaming him for the loss of his mine and assets.

Joseph jumps at the chance to return to an active role in mining. He knows Ellen will approve of any activity that will keep him away from the pub. Moreover, he can walk to work and will be home every night. He is even more delighted when he learns Joe and his future son-in-law, Norman Burrows, an experienced mine accountant, are shareholders.

The mine is acquired and Joseph starts work in September 1907, with the blessing of Ellen. By November, an optimistic first meeting of shareholders hears the new shaft has been sunk to a depth of 135 feet and high grade leaders have been intersected. The perspective of Joseph is different. The rapid early digging is above the water table and purchase of the pump is deferred 'until it is needed.' Now that water is encountered, de-watering of the shaft is being conducted with a kibble, the large heavy duty bucket, normally used for raising broken rock and personnel, instead of a pump. This system cannot cope with the amount of water flooding into the shaft. Moreover, it is labour-intensive and dangerous. A man clinging to the ladder at the side of the shaft, guides the kibble to the sump, tipping it so it fills with water, then signals for it to be hoisted. At the surface, two men swing the kibble onto a trolley, pushing it to the edge of the shaft dump and tipping the water into a gutter leading it away from the shaft infrastructure.

By February 1908 the shaft reaches a depth of 190 feet and the company needs more funds. Water is by now a major problem but requests by the mine-workers for the installation of a pump are refused, owing to lack of funds, even though the State has contributed 1,000 pounds towards pumping expenses. Winter comes and for five straight days a chill south-east wind blows thick clouds laced with drizzly rain from the Great Australian Bight, followed by three days of gale force, cold southerly winds, direct from Antarctica, accompanied by driving rain and occasional hail. It is an unusually long period without the winter sunshine which makes the Goldfields such a pleasant place to live.

The winder is housed in a 'lean-to.' Joseph has a roof over his head but this is no protection from the bleak weather that has prevailed for more than a week. Joseph alternates between driving the winder, where he is exposed to the elements and stoking the steam engine, which causes him to sweat profusely. It is not surprising when he takes ill. Confined to his bed, he is wracked at first with severe pneumonia. Once the worst of the fever has subsided, he is so weak he cannot spend more than a few minutes on his feet before returning to his bed. Joseph never goes back to work.

May is married to Norman Burrows in April 1908 and they go to live in Bonnie Vale. In a studio photo of the wedding group, Joseph is sitting by the bridal party with a full head of short-cropped, white hair and white tips to his bushy moustache. He is clearly still ill from his misadventure at the Redemption mine, as evidenced from somewhat sunken eyes. May, at 23 years of age, is a pretty bride with a petite figure, pleasant facial features and bobbed hair. Norman is tall, lean and clean-shaven with wavy short hair and looks younger than May. The groom's father is a tall, patrician figure with dark hair and moustache. A wedding breakfast for seventy guests is in the St Andrews Parish Hall. Ellen's gift to the couple is a set of table and house linen, Joseph's gift, a piano.

Marriage of Norman and May Burrows, Coolgardie, April 1908. Rear from left: Unknown, Norman, May, Robert Burrows. Front from left: Joseph, Unknown, Mrs Burrows Snr.

Meanwhile the fortunes of the Redemption Mine continue to fade. A Cornish lift pump, a device that lifts water in a series of stages, is installed in October 1908. New stages can be added as the mine deepens but it is unable to cope with major water inflows. After many problems, including an accident and a fire, the shaft reaches the 300 feet level in January 1909 and development of the level commences. In February, the development breaks into old workings, causing the mine to flood again. A shareholder meeting in

April reports the company has debts of over 4,000 pounds but the directors remain confident of a profitable outcome. The Minister for Mines, Mr Gregory, visits Coolgardie in July to attend a race meeting. In the evening the Redemption directors and mine manager button-hole the Minister at the Victoria Hotel to explain the current 'financial or rather unfinancial state of affairs.' The Minister offers to pay 25 per cent of the cost of pumping provided the company pays for the rest. However, the company lacks the funds to pay the remaining 75 per cent of pumping costs.

The mine manager asks the Minister, 'What would become of the mine if this arrangement were not carried out and the mine becomes flooded?'

The Minister replies emphatically, 'The Government will foreclose the mortgage and will find some other party who will do so.'

In August, an extraordinary meeting of shareholders takes place to consider whether to wind up the company or seek to raise more capital. A number of directors resign following this meeting and Joe finds himself in the uncomfortable position as a Director of a company in financial distress. The Board proposes to issue preference shares to raise funds but it is to no avail. The government forecloses on its 1,000 pound debt and advertises for a tribute party to take over the Redemption Mine.

Joseph is unaware of these developments. In May 1909, after a summer of recuperation, he begins to feel a little stronger and arises to have breakfast with Ellen. It is a Sunday and Ellen leaves him sitting in the warmest spot in the house, by the kitchen stove, to go to church. When she returns mid-morning, she finds him sitting in the same comfortable chair with his eyes closed and a serene expression on his face. She smiles at the sight and just as she does so, his eyes open and he smiles back at her.

'I was just thinking back at what a good life we have had,' he says. 'We found gold, ran a hotel, tried farming, raised a family and watched our children grow up and make their way in the biggest state in the world. This state of Western Australia is so big and unknown, it could turn out to be a mineral treasure house in the future. If I had my time over again, I wouldn't change a thing. The best thing I ever did was marry you.'

Ellen shrugs and busies herself, stoking the fire and making scones to serve with morning tea. This is a Sunday tradition. Ellen lathers the cooked scones with butter while they are still piping hot, so it melts immediately. Joseph likes to add Ellen's home-made quandong jam, made with fruit from a native tree common in the Goldfields, to his scones. Ellen places the scones, jam and two cups of tea on a stool placed next to Joseph's armchair and pulls up a kitchen chair so she can sit next to him.

They finish their morning tea in contented silence. Joseph reaches out and takes her hand and closes his eyes again, seemingly resuming his reverie. After some minutes, she senses him slightly quiver and his grip on her hand loosens.

Joseph is no more.

Epilogue

Following Joseph's death, Ellen wrestles with a new dilemma, what to do with the mortal remains of her husband of forty one years? His death was sudden and although not entirely unexpected, he had left no instructions. Joseph had never relinquished his affiliation with Roman Catholicism. Throughout his life, although he seldom attended Mass, he would often enter the Roman Catholic churches in both Stawell and Coolgardie and either sit in contemplation or indeed, pray and he had suffered for this. Some members of those churches were openly hostile to Joseph because he had married a protestant and worse, allowed his children to brought up as protestants. Despite Ellen's frequent urgings, he had declined to worship with her and the children in the Church of England. She reasons that people of his own faith community did not extend love to him during his life, so why should she go to request an unfamiliar Catholic priest to bury him? The funeral service is much the same in all Catholic churches and most of the people attending will be Church of England, so why not ask the rector of St Andrews to conduct the service? Perhaps she can achieve after his death what she was unable to do while he was living. To Ellen's mind, this is an act of love.

Joseph is buried in the Church of England section of the Coolgardie cemetery. The mourners are mostly extended family and friends but include a large contingent of the Amalgamated Certificated Engine Drivers' Association.

A month after the funeral, Joe's second son, Stan, sees a cobble of laminated quartz amongst the white, bucky quartz edging one of the garden beds at his grandmother's house. He is only six years old at the time but is already fascinated by rocks, so he takes it and adds it to his collection. Years later, training as an assayer at the Coolgardie School of Mines, he decides to test some of the rocks in his collection for gold. He breaks the cobble of laminated quartz into two equal pieces. He tests the first half of the quartz sample by fire assay, the standard technique he is learning. This shows the quartz is rich in gold. He crushes one half of the remainder with a pestle and mortar. He agitates and swirls the crushed rock with water in a panning dish and after discarding the top layers of light material he is left with the denser granules. With a careful rocking action, he isolates the heaviest of these in a tail at the bottom of the dish. To his astonishment, the tail is long and golden, consisting of very fine particles, almost microscopic, of pure gold!

'If only Grandpa had told him where that piece of laminated quartz had come from!'

Joe loses money in most of his mining ventures. In 1915, he forms a syndicate with two other Coolgardie businessmen, Cashen, manager of Brennan's drapery store and Hanley, a butcher, to back a tribute party on the Bayley's Reward mine. The tributers, McCulloch and Maynard, battle away for several months, receiving 2 pound a week from each of the trio of businessmen, in search of a rich patch of gold that McCulloch had been confident would be found.

One day he approaches Joe with a sorrowful expression and says, 'I was wrong. I'm sorry but there is no gold. There is no point in my taking more of your money so if you will give me a clearance, you can stop your payments.'

After getting a clearance from Joe, he goes to Cashen, who also gives him a clearance. It is a different story when he approaches Hanley, who refuses to give a clearance. Hanley later reproaches Joe and Cashen for giving in so easily. About three weeks later the three left in the syndicate share profits of some £3,000 each. To add salt to the wound, it transpires McCulloch has been selling gold to Norm Green, a Kalgoorlie assayer that Joe had helped set up in business.

In 1924, when Coolgardie is becoming a ghost town, Joe dismantles his house, puts it on the train to Perth and rebuilds it on one of the first vacant blocks in Waratah Avenue, Dalkeith.

Joe's photograph is included with the Pioneers and Prominent Citizens of Coolgardie in its heyday, in a composite photograph displayed in the bar of the Denver City Hotel at the time of writing.

Joseph and Ellen's oldest daughter, Maria, who had married long-term family friend Alf King gives birth to one son, Raymond, whose life is blighted by mental health problems.

The Mazzucchelli and Downes partnership is dissolved in 1912, when Sam Downes leaves to set up business in Albany. Matt Mazzucchelli assumes sole control of the jewellery business in Boulder now known as Mazzucchelli's. He opens another shop in Kalgoorlie but in 1920, at a time of depression in the Goldfields, moves the business to the corner of Hay Street and Central Arcade in Perth. The business expands in Perth and to Geraldton under Matt's sons, Harold and Edwin and is eventually sold in 1996, after some 93 years as a family business. The Mazzucchelli's clock is returned to Kalgoorlie by his grandchildren in 1968, where it now hangs outside the Kalgoorlie Museum.

Albert is content to earn a wage as a barber in Coolgardie until early 1909, when he goes into business in Kellerberrin as a tobacconist and barber. He marries Rebecca. Their only child, a daughter, dies as a result of a tragic accident while still an infant. Albert later moves his business to Narembeen.

In 1917, Herb walks off his Hampton Downs property, defeated by the prolific box poison bush, which kills many of his sheep. His sister, May Burrows, helps him financially to re-establish his family of five daughters in the embryonic local government area of Gosnells. He continues his interest in local government throughout his life and a park in Gosnells bears his name.

May and Norman Burrows and their two daughters, Mavis and Edna, move to Tasmania. Mavis marries Stuart Dunbar and together they have two daughters, eventually moving back to Western Australia. Edna never marries but returns periodically with her widowed mother to visit the Mazzucchelli family in Perth.

A curious fact. Joseph and his descendants spell Mazzucchelli with two 'c' whereas Matteo's descendants spell Mazzuchelli with one 'c'. Why is a mystery. The official records in Poschiavo have the family name as 'Mazzucchelli' and this is how Joseph's name is spelled on his emigration document. It seems Matteo dropped a 'c' somewhere between Prada and Victoria. All formal references to Joseph and Matteo in Stawell have their names spelled differently despite the fact they are brothers.

Ellen moves to Boulder and then Subiaco, where she dies in 1927. She continues to serve the Anglican Church throughout her life and is an active worker for the Red Cross during World War I. Anecdotally, she is known as a stern and severe old lady, a somewhat fearful figure to her grandchildren. Her reaction to her grandson, Edwin, when he breaks his leg riding a billy-cart is typical, 'What an expense you have cost your poor father!'

Acknowledgements

This story is based on historical research relating to my great-grandfather's life as an immigrant, prospector and miner. The known events in my great-grandfather's life and as much anecdotal material as I have been able to obtain, have all been included in the story. I have filled the many and substantial gaps by imagining a narrative, drawing on my own experiences in mineral exploration and mining and industry characters I have met in the course of more than fifty years. I have drawn background material from many sources. The original records of the Mazzucchelli family were from the official records of births and deaths at the Ufficio dello Stato Civile, Records Office, in Poschiavo in 1990. The Stawell Historical Society supplied much information on the Mazzucchelli and Mazzuchelli families in Stawell as Joseph and Matteo, respectively, spelled their names.

I apologise unreservedly if any reader finds my representation conflicts with their personal knowledge, which was not available to me at the time of writing. My aim is to tell a story about the excitement and romance of prospecting and mining. To that extent, I have unashamedly invented some adventures that make my great-grandfather's life seem less humdrum than it probably was.

I am overwhelmingly grateful to Jenny Kohlen, like me, a great-grandchild of Joseph, for many of the few anecdotes I have, as well, much factual, historical research. The late Stan Mazzucchelli, who was Joe's second son, used to visit me when I lived in Kalgoorlie in the 1960s and '70s and later in Perth in the '80s and loved to reminisce about his early days in Coolgardie. I have used my notes from his visits.

My gratitude to Mardi May and the Past Tense writers' group, part of the Katharine Suzannah Prichard Writers' Centre, for their writing tips and gentle urging. A special thanks to my wife Brenda, for her loving support of my crazy ventures over more than sixty years.

Bibliography

The Following publications have provided valuable insights:

C.E. Sayers. (1966) *Shepherd's Gold: The Story of Stawell.* F.W. Cheshire: Melbourne.

Geoffrey Blainey. (1963) *The Rush that Never Ended: A History of Australian Mining.* Melbourne University Press.

S.T. Gill & N. Chevalier. (1857) *Victoria Illustrated 1857 &1862* with Introduction and notes by W. H. Newnham. Lansdowne Press.

Robert Pascoe and Frances Thomson. (1989) *In Old Kalgoorlie.* Western Australian Museum.

Thomas Keneally. (2016) *Australia: A Short History.* Allen & Unwin.

Stevan Eldred-Grigg. (2008) *Diggers, Hatters and Whores: The Story of the New Zealand Gold Rushes* (Random House New Zealand)

Joseph Gentilli. (1989) *Swiss Poschiavini in Australia.* Geowest 25.

Jacqueline Templeton. (1998) From an Italian Swiss Valley to Australia: A Study on Emigration and the Home Community. *Aust J. Politics & History:* Volume 44 Number 1, pp. 49-67.

Lynne Stevenson. (1989) *The Coolgardie International Exhibition, 1899.* Studies in Western Australian History, No. 10, Apr 1989: 100-106

Nancy Hobson and Dorothy Saunders. (1970 circa) *The Church of England on the Goldfields: The First Twenty Years.*

Milton Keynes UK
Ingram Content Group UK Ltd.
UKHW050224250324
439991UK00015B/1870